Power of self-knowledge is the most
treasured jewel for your soul.

The Mirror is You

Siddiya Swift

VIBEXPRESS PUBLISHING, LLC
CONYERS, GA

Vibexpress Publishing, LLC
P.O. Box 83083
Conyers, GA 30013
Phone: 770-388-0769 Fax: 770-388-0253
email: publishing@siddiyaswift.com

www.siddiyaswift.com

Edited by Eddye Gallagher
Book design by Stacy Luecker
www.essexgraphix.com
Cover illustration by Rickey R. Washington Jr.
www.energyexerteddesigns.com   email: rickeyw@aol.com

ISBN: 0-9728762-0-0
Library of Congress Control Number: 2003101768
Printed in the United States of America.

First printing, Vibexpress edition, April 2003

DEDICATION

This book is dedicated to the Source of all that is. To my mother and father, Ann and Lee, thank you for the gateway to experience life. To my sisters, Lisa and Wendi, we will be together eternally no matter what. I love the both of you. To Royce, Myles and Andre, you are the best nephews anyone could wish for. To a special niece, Latoya, make sure you complete your mission. I love you dearly. To other family and friends, I thank you for sharing your light as well as your darkness. Last but not least, to the Funk Master, who is an amazing, loving and compassionate soul partner—we crossed paths exactly when we were supposed to. I thank you for your sparkling energy through self-expression of fertile words, concrete work, endurance and wholesome love. May all of you reach your goals. Our ancestors are we, and we are they. May each one of us walk the journey in light and in darkness so we can learn who we really are through what we express. Home is in the soul of you and me.

In loving memory of Monica Goree Adams, I miss you, girl; my grandfather, Carl Fraction, I won't forget all the things you said over and over; my ancestors; spiritual teachers, known and unknown, thank you for communicating with me. I realize that death is only a channel to another form of life, and I know you are still here fully in another creation.

CONTENTS

ACKNOWLEDGMENTS

First and foremost, I would like to thank my editor, Eddye Gallagher, for polishing and honing this book. I appreciate your honesty and integrity.

Stacy Luecker, the best book cover graphic designer and typesetter on the planet. Your talent is precious. Keep doing what comes to you naturally.

I would like to thank my mother, Ann M. Burchett, for being a loving and supportive guide. Your motherly nature is what keeps me moving forward. I love you!

And to my precious companion, Rickey, thanks for your open-mindedness and loving support. Your love has been original, and I am grateful for who and what you are.

Life is blood that flows like unseen matter.
The light reflects its fire, penetrates green
sunrise and sunset. Explosive is this energy.
Does it cease to exist in life, or does it contain
the fire and speed higher? Let's rest upon life,
light, and shadow hour, ascend into all
dimensions and rise, rise higher.

When I look at trees of life and see how
strong the branches are, I stare at how the
wind makes these branches grow. The gliding
wind from time to time sails like a storm;
trees of life with branches admire the breeze
wherever it goes. Each tree branch sails and
flows with the wind as if it already knows
how fast the wind will blow.

INTRODUCTION

How many of you have looked in the mirror and counted the times you've really seen yourself, the real you? I'm sure not many. Not even I have done such a thing. If you really think about that question, you'll probably wonder why I would form such a thought. Well, first of all, our souls are at stake when we don't know who we really are. Second, we are at a disadvantage to ourselves when we don't know who we divinely are from within. And, third, we must see that we are bigger than what we think and really begin to look for an enhanced purpose while we're here on planet Earth.

You may not know this, but we are living in an era that what we think or don't think of ourselves matters. As we wake up to the fact that we are in a learning process of conscious evolution, each of us as individuals has a responsibility to develop a state of mind that will fulfill all aspects of who we are. Quite often, we are slaves to our negative thoughts, projections, beliefs, experiences and destructive behavioral patterns that we are powerless to see that what is in our minds determine the path we will create. Many of us are in search for a purpose and a better life, but, in order to attract better, each of us must be willing to be what we what to experience. To know who you truly are, you must become aware that your consciousness is your mirror. You must know that what you think in your mind are the experiences you will encounter. As soon as you recognize this, perhaps you will move your mind toward a consciousness of good to manifest experiences of good.

If not, there are plenty of energy thieves in this world who will prey on you because you don't know who you truly are. Look around! People are killing themselves and one another. Many are dependent on drugs, stressed out, outraged and confused, and they don't know why. A large number of people are in family confrontations, rude to their friends and feeding off one another's weaknesses. Some folks are suffering and contracting diseases because they don't have control of themselves sexually. A large number of adults and children are missing, nowhere to be found. Numerous people lack money for food and shelter. And, masses need additional self-love, peace, serenity, joy and a better life. If you look around, you can see that energy thieves prey off of those who don't know themselves. Look around, the mirror is staring you right in your face.

This is a time when one can no longer continue to blame others for burdens, depravities, ignorance and deceptions. Since each soul must learn to love unconditionally in order to find his or her way home, there comes a point in life when you must decide to shape and mold yourself for the betterment of your soul. After all, the life you save may be your own.

When I became aware of how much love I wasn't giving to others and to myself, I decided to look in the mirror and closely examine the soul of the real me. I started to look at who I really was and where I was going. I started to acknowledge that I was tired of constantly allowing my shallowness and fear-based thoughts to cause me to lose precious energy and strength. I was exhausted, weary and emotionally drained by my own insecurities and from allowing others to dump their issues on me. I was in a hopeless state of mind and needed to over correct my thoughts to higher realms of spiritual principles that would direct my path to a broader and deeper consciousness of self-support. When I began to look in the mirror, the real me revealed itself.

In studying my mirror, I realized that I have choices. I can either shatter my mirror or shape it into a diamond piece. Or I can create false images or get down to the nakedness of my being and relate to my soul. We each have so many choices that we sometimes miss the clarity of what is vital for our mirror to reflect, in the highest realm of self-discipline, self-mastery and self-love.

Few of us look in the mirror and truly watch where we are going with our thoughts; others don't know where to go with theirs, and most people are blurred by their mirror because they don't even see that their thoughts are a mirror reflection of who they are.

To the people who really look in the mirror, what do you see? To the people who don't look, why aren't you looking? And to the people who look, but only look for false images, what are you seeing?

This book is meant to help souls on their journey in life. Every day we are faced with so many challenges, life-altering shifts and confused states of affairs that we can't see what mirror we wish to create. One particularly challenging task is facing ourselves in the mirror. My vision is that on your journey in life, you have found this book and that it will help you to look into your mirror and face the real you. We all need help maintaining self-awareness and self-empowerment. You don't have to read this book in order; you can open it any moment to any page and get something of true meaning from it. I would like to congratulate you already on your journey to self-awareness. You should read *The Mirror Is You* as many times as you need and apply the principles to your life for the strengthening of your soul. When you begin to master you, your whole being comes right into alignment. Think about it. You are here for a purpose. How long will it take you to look into your mirror? The mirror is a bright light of love. May this love always be you! The choice is yours. This book is my gift to you, the real you.

With Love,
Siddiya Swift

CHAPTER 1

THE NEED OF ACCEPTANCE FROM OTHERS VS. SELF-ACCEPTANCE

By facing the truth of who you are, there is more meaning to life.

THE NEED OF ACCEPTANCE FROM OTHERS

Acceptance is the act and fact of being approved of. Why do we expect others to accept us? How do we reprogram our different beliefs and behavior traits about needing others to accept us? And how do we let go of second guessing ourselves when we must rebuild and trust our own inner abilities.

How you begin the journey will depend on what you want to accept from others and what you expect from them concerning you. Some people reject accepting things as they are, and that's okay. Some people accept things just as they are, and that's okay, too. The real question is how can we accept ourselves first and be at ease without the approval of others?

We accept ourselves first by looking in the mirror of our own self, who we really are, not by pleasing someone else's view of how they think we should be. We accept ourselves by expanding our own conscious mirror with bigger ideas and concepts, not by someone else's concepts of how they think we should be, and we accept ourselves first by accepting our highest and greatest capabilities. When we begin to create our own experiences

1

through focusing on a higher state of consciousness, we will have to recognize the difference between needing approval from others and embodying self-approval.

In spite of the ways others would like for you to be, there is no other person who can mirror the positive qualities you have in your mirror. I have come to know that you have to return to you. I have discovered that most people are not willing to comprehend who they are, yet they try to look in the mirror of your mind and alter you in their likeness. Because our appearances change and things come and go, you can't limit your potential or restrict yourself for another. Our words, views, choices and decisions are what we are responsible for when we are looking in the mirror, but many of us have been and still are so conditioned to needing someone else's opinion that we are unable to think for ourselves. I'm not implying that you should not listen to other's viewpoints. But when you're accepting other's beliefs, you must first ask yourself how this would affect you mentally, emotionally, physically and spiritually.

There's nothing wrong with acceptance; in fact, acceptance is good for healing and acknowledging our behavior traits. It can help you to build upon becoming a better person by overcoming jealousy, anger, impatience, fearfulness, shame, negativity, arrogance or any other discomforting emotion. It can allow you to make decisions and recognize what it is that you need to gain knowledge of. Acceptance can help you distinguish what mirror you want to create for yourself: perhaps a diamond-cut mirror shape, a sparkling glass mirror or a crystal-clear one. Whatever choice you make, the mirror you choose is what acceptance is truly about. But be conscious of the mirror you choose to form each day and be willing to change that which is not needed in your life to better your soul.

Look in the mirror

Did the need of acceptance from others happen all of a

sudden? Did needing acceptance happen when we were born? Are we mistaking this need for love? Is it attention we want? Or could it be we are here to gain knowledge of ourselves through others? These are some of the many questions we could ask in order to choose the mirror we want and rise above the reasons we need approval from others.

In our lives, we have needed our families for support, friends for advice and teachers to assist us in becoming leaders so we can lend a helping hand. And most of us still need their positive assistance, encouragement, service and aid. But I have discovered that communicating with family, friends, teachers or people we don't know very well can be difficult at times, especially if we allow them to throw us off our path of what we choose to create for ourselves in our mirror.

When we lack clarity concerning our goals and ourselves, we tend to open the door for others to make the final decisions for us, and this interference sometimes clouds our perception even more. We become so overly emotional about what others think we should be doing and how they view us and think of us that we lose focus on what we should be doing for ourselves. We don't look in the mirror to recover who and what we are. We allow others' views to be forced on us because we don't think we have the ability to be conscious of what we can do for ourselves; therefore, we confuse the need for acceptance from others and self-acceptance as being the same, when in fact they are different.

Do not take what I'm saying here the wrong way. It is pleasing to have others support you when you need their guidance or assistance, but it is also easy to stray away from the uncertainty of your own thoughts and goals for others' thoughts and goals. Just be aware! Don't lose sight of what you're trying to accomplish. Look in the mirror; remain focused, and do what is best for you. The bottom line is this: it's your life to experience, and you have free will to do so.

My experiences have led me to go beyond the reasons why we project images in our minds about needing acceptance from others. First and foremost, we are not as knowledgeable about the true identity of ourselves, and we don't know how to love ourselves, let alone our families, or friends, so how can we accept anyone for who they are when we must first acknowledge what we are.

In acknowledging what you are, you must be honest with yourself and not be afraid. If you are the type of person who gets angry easily, you need to find a constructive way to deal with your anger. Perhaps there are some underlying inner issues that you haven't confronted. If you are a person who pretends because you don't know how to deal with people, you need to be straightforward with yourself. Perhaps there are some internal problems you need to confront within your own mental mirror image. And if you are a type of person who complains too much, stop wasting your energy in complaining; instead, you have to become what you want another person to be. Let the experiences you encounter on an everyday basis through family, friends and other people be the lessons you need to learn the most. I believe all actions and attitudes from others reflect how you feel about yourself. When you look in the mirror, you must be willing to confront and release anger, arrogance, complaints and other negative emotions. If not, people will only show you what you feel about yourself.

I have found that when we are too shy, timid or fearful to tell others that their way of thinking is offensive to us, we withdraw and feel less about ourselves because we really do care what others think. There's nothing wrong with caring about how others think of you; however, it is just as significant to care about thinking of yourself.

Remember this: you can accept, detach or reject any condition, circumstance, idea, relationship, event, or behavior, whether it's your own or someone else's. The decisions regarding what you accept or will not accept are yours to make.

Don't waste energy being concerned about what others think of you, not even if the person is someone in your family. Be cautious with your energy and you'll conserve most of it for concentrating on how to strengthen your mirror first. Then once you get yourself together by being attentive to your divine mirror, you'll be less likely to worry about how others think and feel about you. On top on that, you'll bond better with your family and others because you'll be less emotional about what people think of you.

Some of you may be thinking that I'm not close to my family and that I don't care to be. As I pointed out before, you may choose what you want in your life, but you have no choice when it comes to family; like it or not, you're stuck. If you're in a situation where you really don't care for your family or someone else that you know, re-evaluate your emotions and allow love to kill the hate in you. You must be the bigger person in all that you do, especially when working to develop your soul.

As I said before, you must look in the mirror and mold a perfectly honed cut glass for you. All you have to do is ask questions because countless answers are waiting for you.

We can project different mirrors in our mind about needing acceptance from others. Many of us are so attracted to cracked mirrors with broken personalities we disregard our own damaged mirror of multiple personalities. Is it because we prefer our fragmented mirror, or is it because we don't know how to throw away the broken mirror and get another one?

When you really look in the mirror, you can recognize the frame of your mirror through the different kinds of people you pull toward you. All you have to do is pay close attention to the people you draw to you. You have the yes people who'll agree to anything, yet they rarely deliver. You have the no people who are negative, pessimistic and quick to point out why something won't work. Worse, they're inflexible and resist change. They can throw a wet blanket over an entire organization. Then there are the know-it-alls, experts on everything. They can be arrogant, and they usually have an opinion on every issue. Yet when they're wrong, they ignore differences of opinion or become defensive.

There are also the complainers. Is anything ever right with these people? You get the feeling they'd rather complain about things than change them. Even though they're often right, their negativity and nitpicking turn people off. I know I had to remove this one out of my mirror carefully.

The passives are easy to spot with their expressionless faces, their weak handshakes and their blank stares. Avoiding conflict and controversy at all costs, these people never offer ideas or opinions and never let you know where you stand. Then you have the dictators, who bully, interrogate and intimidate. They're blunt to the point of being insulting. They're constantly demanding and brutally critical. These folks can cause ulcers if you let them. Do not take the different personalities' mirrors we face everyday in the wrong way. I do not hate people, nor am I speaking badly about them. I just want people to see that each of us can be difficult in our mirrors, particularly when we live in fear. That is why it is so important to be watchful and to focus on forming your mirror than to feel as though you have to need someone else's mirror outlook.

When you don't look in the mirror of the real you, the majority of the time you tend to gravitate toward the views of others concerning how you should be, and this tendency can make you react in an adverse way without even realizing it.

Throughout our lives, people constantly exchange energy with each other, and in some cases, we take advantage of another without noticing how precious each person really is. Here is how it happens: the family is your first experience in sharing energy. You take in healthy and unhealthy qualities from them. Depending on who you are, what you can handle and what your situation is, you absorb either most of the negative attributes or most of the positive attributes from them. Since, we weren't taught in the beginning how to balance out our good and bad opposing personalities, we developed an unbalanced nature, and this is why some of us are discordant and complicated people. Perhaps, it's time to gain a little more control over yourself by relinquishing negative thought waves.

As you read, you will come across Chapter 8: *Mental Battle vs. Balance the Forces of Nature*, so you can see how an unbalanced nature works.

To what extent would you remain absorbed by the energy of others and take on their mental outlook in what they believe will work for you? What mind-set would make you say, "No, I will do what is conducive for me?" In what way would you articulate to others that their way isn't for you? These are more of the questions we could ask ourselves when we look in the mirror. Nevertheless, I'm certain many of us are still struggling with carrying the baggage of not fitting other people's measurements. Maybe, in those bags are your past childhood feelings of not measuring up. Possibly, in those bags are your teenage years of overreaction and exaggerated situations. Perhaps, in those bags are your adult growing pains. At any rate, the real question is do you really think that you can't measure up? If you think you can't measure up, you have to ask yourself whom you are trying to measure up to. Is it for you or someone else?

Don't be afraid to be firm and let others know what isn't or is working for you. Don't be afraid to question others when they want you to believe in them. And mainly, don't be afraid to accept yourself first. Put an end to needing acceptance from others and really begin to have the power and control over you. Shape the world you want in your mirror and see how long it will stay that way.

Many of us don't know how to control our daily thoughts
and activities. We blood suck off each other because we want to
be fixated on what we think can save us. Instead of dealing
with our own baggage, we look for others to do it for us.
Instead of withdrawing from clinging, we run to others and
hide our problems through them.

Furthermore, whenever you immerse your being in situations
and certain individuals from whom you may soak up unwholesome
interactions, you may take on some of their attributes, such as
violence, disrespect, theft, lies and other useless, distracting
influences. In order to form a diamond-shaped and crystal-
clear mirror, you must be willing to make clear to you how to
gain control of yourself by non-attachment, which is nothing
more than detaching yourself and eliminating emotional reactions
to situations and certain people.

My focal point is this: some people can't cope with what
they absorb because too much hardship can make them act
destructively. And a majority of the time, what they consume
is self-doubt, insecurity, self-hatred, blame, regret and fear;
furthermore, all this does is prolong the war within each person
who chooses to continue to have broken mirrors. The cycle never
stops until each individual takes responsibility for his or her own
actions.

Don't be afraid to deal with your baggage because you are
the only one carrying it. Let your growing adult life be the
happiness or unhappiness of what you wish for yourself. And,
remember to be knowledgeable of you; however, be polite to
others in the process of digesting more positive energy than
negative energy.

It doesn't matter what age you are when you look in the
mirror. The soul is here to improve. After you master one lesson,
develop the skill and move on to the next. It doesn't matter what
people say about you; it's what you think that really matters. Just

take time out to become aware of the fact that your experiences are mirror reflections of who and what you are. Family and acquaintances are here to assist you to overcome what it is that you need to be taught the most, whether it is something you choose to experience or not.

Don't mistake experiences you must grasp through others as needing them. Realize that in the end, your thoughts and actions are what you will produce through your mirror.

The reality of my traumatized mirror set in early for me. It can happen to anyone consciously or unconsciously. I had no idea that I would have to carry a traumatized mirror with me years later. I can laugh about it now, but it wasn't funny back then.

I was nine years old, in the fourth grade and attending elementary school in Chicago. The memory is still clear. It seemed most of the girls in my classroom were developing fast, except me. I was skinny and flat chested, and I wore long johns underneath my pants in the summertime so I could look like I had a big butt. The boys in our classroom only wanted to hang around girls who had bigger breasts and bigger butts. It didn't matter how nice you were; the only thing that mattered was having a shape. My thoughts became centered around how the boys viewed me and how some of the more attractive girls were getting their attention.

One of my friends, Tracy Blue, had just started to develop—physically and emotionally—but I wanted to ignore that change because I was accustomed to our playing toys together. I was not thinking about wearing sexy clothes or makeup. To keep up with my classmates and gain attention from the boys, I decided to change. The preconceived thought of not being accepted from the boys back then had consumed me like a vacuum cleaner picking up trash. I felt like a loser because I didn't want to accept the fact Tracy and many of the other girls were developing fast.

One day while lying in bed, I thought about putting some

tissue in my bra. I jumped out of bed and went quickly through the kitchen into the bathroom to get some tissue. I looked around to make sure that neither my mother nor sister would see the tissue package underneath my arm as I swiftly passed back through the kitchen into my bedroom. I closed my bedroom door, opened the dresser drawer and took out my training bra. When I put on the training bra, it was tight around my chest, perfect to stuff the tissue in my bra and keep it from falling out. I formed the tissue to the size I wanted. When I looked in the mirror, I felt like a new person. I was sitting straight up poking out my chest, thinking to myself, "All the boys are going to like me." Then I thought that if I went to school like this, I would get a lot of the boys' attention.

I went to school the next day and was feeling happy until a little boy came up to me during recess and said loudly while pointing his finger, "Those aren't your breasts. You have tissue in your shirt." As the boys began to gather around to look at my fake breasts, I yelled for them all to get away from me. I was so embarrassed. My little ego was shattered the rest of the day. All I had wanted was to satisfy this need of acceptance from the boys. I also had wanted to fit in with the rest of the girls who had shapely bodies. Somewhere in my undeveloped mind, I thought no one would have recognized the tissue in my bra. That illusion I created for myself at nine left me feeling insecure for many years.

My mother used to tell me all the time, "You look nice! Don't worry about being small; you are fine just the way you are!" No matter how many times she told me, I just didn't believe it. No matter what I did physically to make myself look a certain way or how nice I was, there was still something missing within my being, and that attitude was not changing my mirror to another mold. All of the experiences of my teen-age years and early twenties were painful to some extent. I was still carrying this disease—the need of acceptance from others—because I still hadn't figured out how to accept me just the way I was.

Everything I thought and did was based on how I needed others' acceptance. For example, in my past relationships, I was always the one giving more mentally, physically, financially and spiritually. I would put up with a lot just to be with a man. It didn't matter if the person was abusive or crazy. The first time I was hit by my ex-boyfriend, I actually thought it was okay for him to do that. It seemed to me that he was expressing his love for me. It is absolutely amazing some of the things women and men will do to keep a relationship so they can feel whole when they're living in a destructive state of mind.

When you feel less about you, you attract less to you. I do realize when you're on a mission to fulfill a desire, you're not thinking about the outcome that might hurt you. You are only thinking about getting your fix because that's all you know to do. But that thought process could surely cause you your life. My life wasn't taken from me, but going through my self-caused pain absolutely felt like dying.

When you don't embrace your mirror, you tend to fall for someone else's mirror. And, if you find that your mirror is puzzling to you, create another one so that you can look through a clearer one.

Caught in our own self-inflicted pain, many of us overlook how to craft the mirror we want for ourselves. Others are caught up in crushed mirrors that they don't even realize or know why. None of us are alone in this situation; we all have different mirrors we must adjust. The solution is how skillfully you will choose your mirror—wisely and carefully, step-by-step each day. The universe is always working on our behalf to balance our requests. The key is to develop your being, remove all entrapments in your thinking and draw you to what you mirror your life to be, instead of letting others do it for you.

At an early age, I created a futile idea about myself. I didn't now how to stop my traumatized mirror because I was too busy disregarding the real me. When you really look in the mirror, you will find that the mirror is you and all that you have created. I hope you waste no more energy allowing emotional dissatisfactions with yourself or others to drain you of your divine creative thoughts. Don't forget, every day of our lives we are in contact with others. We are always absorbing one another's energy. Others' energy can sometimes be controlling, passive, persuasive, angry, intimidating, interrogating, aloof, loving, exciting or kind. The ones I have mentioned here are minor compared to all the other types of energy surrounding us.

Millions of people have been programmed to think and do things a certain way in order to feel empowered and to control others. This programming occurs in all your surroundings: families, relationships, friendships, work environments, television and schools. Let your heavenly soul use discernment dealing with your own choices and with people you encounter every day.

Yes, I was a victim. I thought being liked by boys was my ticket to a perfect life, but that proved to be an erroneous belief. You can dress yourself up with makeup, beautiful clothes, jewelry and shoes, and you can add body implants and other stuff, but none of those things mean anything to the soul, which is far more meaningful than material possessions. Your soul definitely deserves better.

When I changed my mirror in an ankh shape, my picture of life became clearer. My soul seemed to draw nearer to who I really was, and the physical stranger in me moved farther from what I thought I knew about myself. Begin now by putting together the type of mirror you want in your life. All it takes is to be honest with yourself and face who and what you really are. If you still do not know what I mean, just look closely at your mirror right now, and ask yourself, "Who am I?" And, if you get no answer, your experiences of your strengths and weaknesses will help you. Sure, I would like to say that this is the last mirror I'm going to alter, but how can I when I'm still changing the mirror everyday? We don't need acceptance from others; what we need is self-acceptance in our own mirrors.

SELF-ACCEPTANCE

Do you know what it's like for you to truly accept everything you have ever done? If you do, congratulations! You have mastered the definition of self-acceptance. If you don't know what it is like, you have a lot of reading and looking in the mirror to do.

Before I begin, I want you to know this first: The most important tool we have within us is the power of thought, the power to make all things possible through what we think in our innermost mind. As noted in the previous section of this chapter, what we mirror in the inner recesses of our mind is what we will do in action. If you don't remember anything else from this book, remember this—our thoughts can destroy us or rebuild our character.

Acceptance is taking the higher journey to get to know the true self

To connect with our higher selves, we have to control our thoughts and focus on pure consciousness. In order for us to focus on pure consciousness, we must be willing to take the higher road to develop lost parts of ourselves by applying the courage to reduce unproductive friction.

I see so many people struggling over differences with partners, friends and families that it is hard for them to see that the same struggle is usually within them. But, if you truly want to liberate yourself from lost parts of yourself, you must be willing to accept the differences in you first by looking through your mirror.

Once you accept your differences and your true higher self

that molds you and attracts others to you, you have shaped a better mirror to see through more clearly.

What are lost parts?

The lost parts are some of our differences that we have to accept to reach to a higher level of being. Instead of arguing over who is "right or wrong, good or bad," recognize why you are both the way that you are. Instead of judging others, remember that all people must develop their souls no matter how their ways are. Be grateful that their ways of being are just as vital for them as yours are for you. In doing this, you can give them a chance to open their latent potential and make bigger who they are.

As long as you can see differences as conflicts, unique viewpoints, emotional feelings and expressed thoughts, you can look in the mirror and really notice that lost parts are mental attitudes, characteristics and behavior traits of who and what we are, whether or not we accept them.

There are no mistakes in life, only experiences

If you can accept the choices you make, then you can accept the experiences you acquire from those choices. For example, suppose you are in a loving relationship with a special person. You give him or her a serious commitment. But by surprise, you find out that he or she is talking bad behind your back, cheating on you and giving you less attention than you deserve. Eventually, however, you realize that it is difficult for you to release this person from your life because you would rather be with him or her for whatever reasons you choose.

We put much effort in unhealthy relationships, obtaining extravagant homes, expensive cars, vacations, but find it impossible to heal our own mind, body and soul. Some of us are more likely to think and trust that the power is outside of us, but it's not. We would rather continue to put up with nonsense than make healthier choices. We would rather behave indecently instead of amicably.

In other words, choices you make in your life can bring on many baffling yet necessary situations. But without accepting, choosing, experiencing and feeling what you are, you will be left not knowing what better choices you can make in the lessons you choose for yourself. Remember that you can replace your mirror as often as you like, but there are no mistakes in life, only experiences. All you should tell yourself in the mirror is to accept and choose wisely.

Loving all parts of ourselves

There is no time limit to how fast we should grow; each person grows at his or her own pace. If you tune in to your higher self, nature will be your assistant as you find the true you. Let nature work for you! All it takes is an open heart, compassion and the ability to allow love to speak to all parts of you.

Loving all parts enables you to love, encourage and support yourself and others. Loving all parts of you connects you with the healing light force within and heals those physical, mental and emotional weak cells that keep you sick. Loving all parts means addressing situations realistically, based on how well you can handle their outcomes. Looking at accepting those parts is part of the recovery process. Thus, if you feel you are doing the best you can every moment, keep doing just that.

If you are facing jealousy or selfishness in your mirror, you basically have to unlearn what you have been taught in your earlier years in order to accept loving all parts. When you're around someone you might be jealous of, express joy for him or her. When someone does not handle things the way you do, do not trouble yourself with the difference; do what is divine for you without being egotistical.

Moreover, do not allow judgment of others to influence

you. Judging people is not a good quality; it is undoubtedly lifeless. Judging people takes more energy because we lose positive energy when sending out negativity. Loving all parts of ourselves is not just about certain attributes of our personalities; it is purely about self-acceptance of who we truly are. We should be accountable for our own thoughts, and before we pass judgment, we should look for the positive in people, but we must make sure we have it in us.

Certainly, we can attest to an aversion toward a number of choices that each and every one of us has made in the past, and our so-called bad experiences do not mean that we can't love this part of us. Learning to accept this part of us through the mirror is a masterwork. Recognizing the parts can help us break negative mental blocks and the vicious cycle of drama in our lives. We can control our emotions by working positively on solving mood swings through loving all parts of ourselves.

Self-approval is progress every day

Are you someone who really looks in the mirror and notices improvements of progress every day? Are you someone who doesn't look in the mirror because you don't care for progress? Perhaps you look in the mirror too much and can't see you're really progressing. Only you can say for sure what type of progressing you are doing.

Numerous people have lost their lives because they weren't making progress toward self-approval. An old friend told me about her cousin who wanted to commit suicide years ago because she was ashamed of how she looked. Apparently, she was mentally and emotionally exhausted from sadness. I mention this because I want you to see how easily you can be fragmented and shifted emotionally when you allow other things to burden you.

When you embrace self-approval each and every day, you

can grasp hold of yourself. You will be less likely to allow overpowering influences to affect you. If you don't know who you are, how could someone else know? I recognize that the media use women to advertise a certain type of look, a practice that can destroy many women who may not have the so-called standard beauty to be accepted in this society. To protect yourself, you must allow the essence within your soul to become important and your conscious to become a distinctive expression of bringing out the ability that makes you greater. If *you* don't care, who will?

I had to learn the hard way to accept myself. I hated my body, the body I love to hate. I suffered the unbearable flat chest and skinny legs. Your being is really about who you are, not what you look like to others. My evolution each day is to remind myself that I am what I say I am; thus, I will accept all that I am, in the progression of what I say I will do. I am the only one who can choose what I know is best for me.

Self-acceptance has always been in you. Somewhere along the way, you forgot to accept you and all that you are; there is no right or wrong in it. It just is. Tap into more of your creative side, let your experiences guide you and be mindful of how you direct your flow. Right now, say to your divine self, "I accept me at all times. I am open to create positive changes for the betterment of my soul while I'm here learning to develop my whole being." In each moment, you are your thoughts, in the mirror of yesterday, today and tomorrow.

CHAPTER 2

SELF-DOUBT
VS.
SELF-CERTAINTY

Establish more wisdom for self and you will feel less confused.

SELF-DOUBT

Self-doubt is being unsettled in opinion or belief. When one's character is attended by uncertainty, the mind is troubled, undecided and hesitant to make sound decisions for itself. Its physical attribute is one of suffering, suppression, aggravation and weakness. We all know that most people have some moments of self-doubt, but what do we do when those doubts and uncertainties steal our day-to-day lives? Do we hold doubts within or do we get to the root and dispel its affliction? Do we keep the faith, or do we work on resolving our doubts by feeding our minds with constructive affirmation for personal growth? Each of us can ask questions about what we doubt, but what will you do to find the answers?

Confront your qualms

In order to confront doubts, we must face up to what we believe in. Many of us believe in people, religion, schools, things of the world and other various public effects, and some of us never question why although there are moments when we may want to question what we believe no matter what our background or spiritual path may be … no matter what our preferences or boundaries. I have found out that most people don't question what they believe. Many people, especially those who slip back into doubts, chain themselves to beliefs and old ideas that keep them from expanding their awareness. But in order to face up to our doubts, we need to reconstruct what we believe and begin to choose new beliefs, perceptions and ideas. So often we get stuck believing in early childhood principles from family, people, religion, schools and things of the world that we get trapped in misguided beliefs and out-dated ideas about ourselves and life experiences. Unfortunately, when we don't pay attention to our recurring thoughts and beliefs that are old, and interfere with our growth process, we may not recognize that some of them no longer support our inner growth and development, which can trigger us to become doubtful and negative. We all know that everyone has ideas, opinions and beliefs, which they are entitled to. However, many of us never first acknowledge our own instinctive power to gain awareness of recognizing what opinions and beliefs would support our personal growth and well-being so we can create happiness and fulfillment and reach our highest and best.

In discussing our doubts and beliefs, there is absolutely nothing erroneous about believing what we choose, nor is it an issue. By going through this process of study, we can determine what may be causing us to doubt. If you opened the door inside of you to take on a different spiritual path, but your family and friends choose another spiritual path and one of your love ones has a hard time with your outlook, how do you win others to your way of thinking without feeling unsure? Do you condemn your-self or feel like you're in the wrong? Do you discuss your final decision with the entire family, or do you make your own final decision? One very testing aspect of being who you are often involves conflict between the emotional and practical sides of your nature, resulting in doubt.

The emotional side of you can agonize over your family's having a tough time accepting the spiritual path you have chosen. The practical side of you has become more aware of a realistic approach to your life through experiences and knowledge. Because you have gained a broader perspective, you understand and accept that what you put forth is acceptable to you no matter what opinion someone else has.

Based on those two sides of you, you are in hesitation. Yet there's a strong will inside that helps you to meet sudden tests, but the qualm inside refuses to think otherwise. Therefore, discord comes from not pointing out the path clearer in your mind based on what you know is right for you.

Sometimes loved ones know how to get inside and agitate us, and we believe their way is the right way. The problem isn't in their viewpoint. The uneasiness is that we must take control of our own lives and honestly stop believing in anyone or anything based on what someone else thinks is true for us. We must get facts based on what will work for us; that way, we will not expect too much of others.

Before you leap into anything—whether it's a new profession, a religious organization, a person's idea or a relationship—have a clear vision about what you wish. Then you'll know exactly what you want without feeling unsettled. There is an old saying: be careful what you wish for, you just might get it. Without a clear vision, you definitely will get what you wish for, along with others' beliefs, attitudes and ideas. So think carefully about what you want in your life; that way you can decrease your doubts.

When your emotions are controlled by self-doubt, explore your feelings and identify with what's really bothering you and become present with the emotions that have surfaced. Then begin to reflect without judging or criticizing yourself. Very often, we aren't aware that we instantly can move beyond self-imposed limited thoughts to create higher levels of consciousness to bring forth that, which will have the greatest healing benefit. The key is to support pure and positive beliefs about yourself that will deliver a more positive and empowering mind. Begin today and open yourself to the experience of productive thoughts that will guide you and uplift your creative potential to emerge. Maintain a balance between your emotional and practical roots by learning the necessary ways to make up your mind and stick to it. Perhaps it is in asking what beliefs or truths are. Maybe it is that we must reverence others' right to their visions as we have our own. Sit quietly and think about what is truly causing you to doubt yourself. Then when it is time for you to change your mirror, you will confront you qualms accordingly.

Find inner peace

No matter how you are positioned in life, in no way should you lose your inner peace. The clearer you are in your thinking, the better you can conquer your self-defeating doubts. When we lack reverence for life and are heavily dependent on our emotions, on others and on attachment to things, how can we believe or trust ourselves? We should know our true selves before we believe.

My wish in grammar school was for boys to notice me. Although I did succeed in getting attention for one day, the result of that wish wasn't healthy for me. In fact, it was upsetting and embarrassing. I doubted my body on the outside because there was no inner peace within. I doubted my body because all of us have been and still are programmed to think about how we should look at ourselves with our ego rather than the power of our spiritual eye. The spiritual eye is our inner knowing of what to create in our lives through the power of our thoughts.

To shape your mind, you need to feed your soul with food of self-knowledge. Fresh information revives your soul, like nutritional food does your body. When you develop your mental existence, new information allows you to think clearer, gain wisdom and carry out insightful thoughts to better your life and support others. As we become aware of our thought patterns, we become conscious of our own emotional, physical and spiritual existence that can support us in understanding more of who we are. Paying special attention to the laws and principles of nature helps you to experience a healthy state of mind especially when you utilize the laws and principles of positive thinking. Self-knowledge gives you the truth to be free to create something new within you. Inner peace comes from knowing those things, particularly when we're working effectively to release a distressed self-imaged mirror.

When I began to look in the mirror, I questioned myself. How could I change a body that was given to me naturally? How could I doubt myself without knowing I was who I was and I would become what I was supposed to become. Why didn't I know as a child that it's not what you have, but what you can create to work for you?

As I've gotten older, I have learned one thing that will never work: you can catch a man by your looks, but you will not keep him because of your looks. Possibly, you can keep him by being in tune with your higher power, being positive in your thoughts, comforting him, always having inner peace and not doubting what you can do. Create situations that are peaceful, and don't be afraid to make corrections. Keep things simple. If you can maintain your inner peace, you can surmount all things.

Build a home of constructive thoughts

No one can pull out anything good in the midst of self-doubt. Suppose you are beginning a passionate relationship; you and the other person are caught in the desire of ecstasy, and you think all is well. But when the tide of ecstasy slows its current, you start to feel comfortable. And just when you thought you were satisfied, the real storm comes along facing you head-on, ready to tear your mind apart. Given that you were so passionate about your relationship, you never thought once about how to build a home of constructive thoughts. Instead, you sacrificed for a physical obsession so you could continue the relationship.

In the beginning, it is sometimes easier to ignore having a loving relationship for a passionate one. It is sometimes hard to see that you can build positive affirmations in your mind as well as give yourself the generosity, consideration and appreciation that you need. But, when the dynamics of a relationship are sustained by physical gratifications first, it is difficult to see what a loving friendship is about. When we refuse to build a home of constructive thoughts, we are left feeling crushed by circumstances of self-doubts.

Some folks build a strong foundation for their home and work hard to maintain that foundation. Others choose to build their home fast because they like the outer appearance better. Some don't care to have a home because they don't want to sacrifice their strength to build one. Before we can build anything, we have to find the strength of our character by first looking in the mirror. Then we can invite others into our homes to share the love of who we are. However, make sure the person you are dealing with also has a home free and clear of self-doubt, and make sure their love is reciprocal.

Since I was never taught how to build a home of constructive thoughts, I doubted everything about my mind, body, spirit and soul. I did not know who I really was. I did not know how to make use of my inner potential. The only thing I was taught to believe in during the early part of my life was the importance of attending school, studying, making good grades and completing college so that I could work for someone else's dreams and "make something of myself." I believed in a system that was unsuccessful to me. I placed my trust in people who didn't warrant it. I believed nothing was possible for me because self-doubt was all I knew. When you don't embrace and build a home of constructive thoughts about yourself, you will be living a lie.

You have the ability to overcome

I attended a small, private Catholic all-girls school in Chicago, and I was embarrassed that I was a so-called below-average student. During orientation, I met some older classmates who had taken a particular English teacher's class. They emphasized how difficult it was to pass her class. Although I tried to avoid her, she taught most of the freshmen and sophomores who were taking English 101, so I was forced to take her class. Because I knew I wasn't good at essay papers, I was afraid to write. My stomach throbbed with pain each time I entered her room. Nearly every day, I knew I was going to be called on to write on the chalkboard. I also knew I'd receive a low grade on my papers. Even though the doubt decreased a little every day and I had the ability to overcome, I was still hesitant.

I realize now that most people are programmed to feel inferior in school. The education system is set up that way. Sometimes you can do your best, but it still isn't good enough. Sometimes you can hide your self-doubt, but it still doesn't help. Sometimes you can think you have failed when, in fact, you have won. You should ask yourself how every situation will affect you. How can you figure out what does or does not work for you? In what way can you overcome your doubts?

Have you ever gotten an essay back that had red marks all over it? Imagine your paper being like that all the time. I became accustomed to self-doubt. I expected not to make good grades. I was more prone to C's, D's and F's on assignments and tests. I doubted myself the entire four years of high school. Making an A or B was far beyond my imagination. How could I have made my mother and teacher happy with good grades when I was never taught to be happy within myself first?

Sometimes, I wonder why children are forced to attend school. It seems more logical to teach your children from home; then, you'll know more about them, and they can learn more about themselves. It would also seem more important to teach your children the many choices they can make for themselves. I'm not against children attending school; however, I don't agree with children being subjected to the errors of grown adults making bad decisions. Have you ever wondered why the system is set up for some to pass and others to fail?

I ask you questions because I want you to think about what you're doing and what you're going to do. It took years before I started to feel comfortable when writing essays. To those of you who might feel intimidated because you are considered what some might call a below-average student, I want to tell you that you are better than what others say and see. You are what you think and know to be true for you. You don't have to discover someone else's dreams. Create your own!

Although I continued my education after high school, I merely attended community colleges to better my reading and writing skills, which had improved during high school. But, I needed something else that was far more important than a college degree: spiritual growth and development. I was capable of going to school at night and working a full-time job, but I continued to doubt my inner potential. When you are around people who doubt, you begin to doubt yourself. I am not blaming others, but remember—you are your environment.

Everyone around me was programmed just like I was. When someone calls you a failure and creates doubt in you, they are also self-doubters. How can anyone be a failure when no one can fall short of what they are created to be? You are what you reflect from the inside; it's neither good nor bad. What you can do is think, study, plan and master the mirror that is you. You can also work toward a goal, accomplish it, push the effort forward and apply it to all things you want to learn in this lifetime. Do the best you can. What you don't get right away, you eventually will with determination. The ship you're directing is your own. Why doubt yourself when you have already won?

You can re-create a mirror by having the ability to overcome. Reconstruct yourself and never doubt what you can do. The truth must be told!

Many say that it's hard to overcome life's challenges. But I say that faith is dead without works. How can you rise above if you believe only in faith and not in your works to take control of your mental, physical and spiritual self? How can you have trust in something when you do not know if it is real? Before you believe in something, find out if it's true so at least you can decide whether you want to put your whole heart into it. And, without a doubt, check it out. You'll be less unsettled, undecided or hesitant to conquer.

Although I became more aware that my life was better throughout my teenage years, there was still barrenness. I was still creating a diagram of recurring self-doubt in areas of my life. Maybe, I allowed the hard-knocks of my life to confine me. Or perhaps, I reacted in such ways that did not seem at all absurd. Even though I studied self-doubt, I was uncertain who I was.

You may wonder why you are living. You don't have any energy to love because you have given in to self-doubt even more than before. When someone tells you something good about yourself, you don't take the compliment because you don't believe it is true. When you look in the mirror, you don't see what's going on inside of you. You don't even see that your life is a mirror reflection of you. All you feel is pain, stress, tension, worry and guilt.

In the case of English 101, every move I made was a four-corner wall of self-doubt until I started my journey within and discovered that I like to read and write. I realized everything I had experienced in the beginning was the first phase of my life story. Those experiences were preparing me for the second phase. You must begin to tap into the design you have created for your life; then and only then, will you see that you have the ability to overcome and create all that is.

Surrender your being to the Creator and let the hand of life guide you. Let all of your divine gifts come forward and ascend into ecstasy, and when you do, you won't have time for self-doubt. You have found your true mission. I recovered my mission in reading. I purposely said recovered because I took back within me what was already there from the beginning. The only reason I didn't see my true mission in the beginning was because my state of consciousness was weakened by self-doubt. Now books have become my best source of information.

Each one of us is an electrifying being; we have the power to create anything if we trust our own divine thoughts. Think about it. When you're busy doing what your mission calls you to do for the betterment of your soul, you don't have time for the negative energy that comes from self-doubt. What you do have time for is replacing the negativity derived from self-doubt with the positivity born from self-certainty.

SELF-CERTAINTY

Self-certainty is the quality of being sure. With self-certainty, you aspire to communicate and express yourself the best you can. It is confidence in yourself. If you knew all you needed was self-certainty to stay in high spirits, what would you do to stay focused?

Find the center

Self-certainty reminds me of the motto "Be all you can be in the Army." I appreciate the motto because I developed my own catchphrase from it: be all you can be for you. Self-preservation is the first law of nature. When you're not being all you can be for yourself, how can you expect to improve and flourish?

When you find the center within your being, you know how to find positive ways to approach your life, accomplish your dreams, better your relationships and improve your self-esteem. One of life's true principles is to love yourself first and set your priorities accordingly to how best you can use your talents. But in order to do make these things come true, you must first be willing to tap into a tremendous amount of inner potential by giving up those things, which keep you down.

When you start to bring out your inner potential, you are less likely to allow pessimistic thinking and situations hold you back. You are preparing to maintain control, which includes being unafraid to face your fears and willing to alter your approach if your path is not centered. By maintaining control, you can deal with your confrontations, be courageous to free and remind yourself that all good things in your life come from the seeds you have sown in your mind. It's okay to have a strong will, to want the focal point. Once you do, you could be in for a wonderful time. Above all, this self-certainty will give you an enormous amount of rejuvenating, powerful energy that is so overwhelming no one or nothing can take it away from you.

The only problem is that you always need to be certain of you and find enough time to effectively become the center of your own paramount reality. Through the mirror, you can naturally choose to open your heart, widen your eyes and accomplish anything you envision. All it takes is to boost your level of wisdom, be receptive and alert to inner guidance and create beauty within yourself. If you are determined, you'll receive self-certainty for the effort you put in today.

Unfortunately, many of us don't take stock in the worthiness and nobleness of our own powerful potential for self-improvement. Instead, we waste precious years trying to find our own center, being ashamed of ourselves, having cranky and critical attitudes and taking advantage of other's weaknesses because we are also weak. Many of us find ourselves in countless things to do and many places to get lost in. We no longer have an inkling about how to become clear.

We would rather make our lives revolve around other people, possessions, addictions, jobs and other impressions, than guide our own unique center. One simple step toward finding your center is to look deep within your soul and shape a mirror that will remind you of your purpose every day.

One day while browsing in Chapter 11 Book Store, I stumbled upon a book titled *You Can Heal Thyself* by Louise Hay. The book's beautiful colors grabbed my attention, but as I began to read the book, I became amazed. The introduction got right to the point about how you can heal your body with your own thoughts. As I squatted right there in the store continuing to read, a thought came to mind. How is it possible for each soul to actually heal its own body? My inner self responded, "Buy the book, and you'll know." As I continued to read, I began to feel an awakening. At the time, I was overwhelmed with doubts. My soul and body were extremely burdened by excruciatingly low self-worth, and I needed a good book to lift my spirit. A feeling of urgency surged through my body, so I had to purchase the book.

When your body and soul become centered, things momentarily seem really strange, especially in the matter of your thoughts. You may want to cry; you may feel sad, or your energy may feel different in some unknown way; however, acknowledge what you feel and be patient with yourself. Recognize when it's time to free your being. One of your biggest uncertainties is facing up to overcome self-defeating thoughts, but try to relax and let your change flow.

When you start to open up, you'll see the beauty in everything—books, people, nature or life itself. You will see that everything is working on your behalf to help boost your self-image. The dormant powers within will begin to awaken, and you will find that you have powers you never even imagined. On top of that, this is not the time to feel rejected or futile. Gather your useful energy, organize your routine and bring your plans to life. This will help to guide you as you center who you really are. When you find out who you really are, self-reliance will begin to take over your being.

In my situation, I began to attract what I was becoming. More books came my way to express more to me, who I was, books like Deepak Chopra's *The Seven Spiritual Laws of Success* and Iyanla Vanzant's *Tapping the Power Within*. The right people came to help me as well. I began putting the old out and moving the new in. The kinetic energy that I felt from my mentors was beyond my mind's eye.

In the past, I couldn't quite figure out why I was always drawn to libraries and bookstores. Now, I recognize that my purpose was shown to me through books. It had been hard for me to catch on to writing essays. I could not see it at the time, but the signs were there. When you begin to look in the mirror, you will see all that is. Your challenges are the doors for far-reaching possibilities, and once you are in the realm of far-reaching possibilities, symbols, signals and message will come to you in action. Action will lead you to recognize opportunity for achievement.

Waste no more time on unimportant idle mental matters. Claim the victory that comes with self-certainty. What you put in your mind becomes a reflection of you. Don't get mad if you don't like the way things are. Get balanced, center yourself within and then transform your dreams to work for you.

You can start right now by training your mind to take in what you really want. Find an outlet that will complement you. Develop a purpose, execute the plan and open up to receive all there is for you, and your self-certainty will shine through. You can do it. Take back what is naturally yours. Stop waiting for something to fall out of the sky. You are the sky; there is no limit to what you can do.

It does not matter how long you take to get focused. As a matter of fact, it's something you have to work at every second of the day. You will get it when the time is right. Just remember to develop your thoughts with positive affirmations. Be careful of what you allow to enter into you. Whether it's toxic people, an unhealthy diet, frustration, fear, guilt, worry or conflict, work to expand your thoughts so you can be certain of who you are. You can't afford to think too long about what you're going to do. You have to be like Nike and "just do it."

Do whatever it takes to maintain your level of self-esteem. Read, write, meditate, rest, exercise or walk. Frequently give yourself a positive talk. Live in a safe, clean, comfortable and peaceful environment if you can. Tell yourself you deserve to have heaven on earth. Get busy and start creating your dreams. Your life is up to you.

But first make certain that you build up the physical and emotional strength you may need when it seems like there is way too much to do and way too little time to do it. Don't worry; you will see yourself being and doing what you never thought you could. This is your moment of self-certainty. All of the good thoughts you've been thinking about yourself will pay off in ways beyond your wildest dream.

Why settle for less anyway when self-confidence is the secret to self-certainty. You know in your soul and spirit, mind and body that you are worthy of the best. You know that the best is you because your mirror has been converted. You're eating healthier foods and doing what it takes to have a stress-free life. You are still and listening to your inner voice. You have found out that you love going to a spa every so often. You see others are only mirrors of you, and you are happy when you look around and see everyone smiling at you.

Be artistic with yourself; there are no procedures or tests to take in order for you to be you. You didn't come with a manual! You are a divine being having a human experience. Lessons are repeated until learned. You can get what you want; your thoughts determine what energies, experiences and people you attract. There is no right or wrong; however, there are consequences. Trust the answers within and know that you are the strength. You construct the pages of your life.

CHAPTER 3

⌒

INSECURITY
VS.
SELF-RELIANCE

The depth of safety is in the soul of our consciousness.

INSECURITY

Insecurity is a mental state of feeling unsafe, nonconfident and apprehensive. Perhaps, most people would probably say that is inaccurate. I, too, would have to agree since insecurity can launch various definitions. And meanings can be different from how we interpret them. That is why we must always investigate for more knowledge until clarification is all-inclusive, sounds true and is clear.

Don't deprive yourself based on what you think a word, a concept or an idea may mean. Be willing to ask questions, search deeper and gain more knowledge. The more you talk about your interest in what you seek to know, the more you'll reinforce the knowledge you want to gain.

Break free

I have noticed that the root of all insecurities is related to lack of knowledge. Most of us think we're independent, reliable and firm. We seem to make our own independent decisions. We seem to be reliable for our families, and we are firm to do what we want for ourselves. For some individuals, this may be more or less true. But what about those unsure moments when you start to worry, fear, expect less and feel you are lacking? How do you handle yourself? Do you break free or engage in the anguish?

There are many ways to break free. One way is to test yourself. When you read an article or a book, let's say you decide not to agree with the writer. However, you take in the good parts of what you want to know, but disagree with the other parts and let them flow out your mind. But, somehow the book adversely affected you making you feel awkward. Do you allow this reaction to affect you miserably, or do you move forward without approving or disapproving?

Many of us are so quick to give our opinions and point our fingers that we miss the core of learning to enhance ourselves. Instead of looking at things from a standpoint of likes or dislikes, start to look at things based on what your soul wants you to know from all angles. Sometimes the things you don't agree with can be the knowledge you need to learn more about yourself.

Become skilled at how to read, listen and benefit from most things but do not allow these things to affect you in an unstable way. Just be willing to look within yourself and ask, "What do I need to double-check from this information I'm getting?" Possibly, it could be for you to study how to discern and distinguish when unwholesomeness is being programmed in your psyche, mainly if it's malevolence being planted in your mind from newspapers, advertisements, videos, movies or music. Perhaps, it could be for you to change for a specific reason. Just because you are connecting with the human race you do not have to be absorbed by the effects of feeling pressured. Utilize who you are and be safe and sound within you own convictions.

For many years, I had been "stuck to my insecurities" by my own lack of knowledge of myself, the setting in which I lived, the circumstances I was exposed to and the people whom I trusted. I had never stopped for a moment to think about how my life related to everyone and everything. I needed to regain full control by not imprisoning my mind to one way of thinking, so I chose to break free and become aware that all things are in my present for me to build on.

The root of affliction

From time to time, I wonder why people are in pain, unhappy and troubled, why some are suffering from anxiety and mental health problems and why the majority of people allow the world of others to eat away at their souls. It is startling to me that we, as humans, are really afraid of our darkness. We are terrified of death simply because we would rather hold on to this world. We seem unreceptive to the total creation of our beingness because we cripple ourselves by pretending that everything outside of us is greater. We are chained to our deficient surface because we don't want to comprehend a vast element of ourselves.

I know one thing for sure: in order for us to unshackle our deficiencies, we must monitor our emotions and work hard to eradicate wretchedness. But first, I want you to visualize yourself naked in front of a mirror and begin to ask yourself these questions: How can I regulate my continuously changing emotions? How can I see in my mind's eye that mood swings are reactions of my feelings, and how can I detect that my emotions are caused by what I think, see, say and do? It is always good to exercise your mind to identify with where you are emotionally, mentally and spiritually. When you are deep-rooted, you are able to recognize rapidly what's concerning you.

The best ways to monitor your emotions is by grabbing control of your thoughts. Remember that not everything in live can be perfect. If you are an envious or resentful person, destroy those thoughts and be glad for your flair as well as the other person's style. If you are a person who can't control your temper, clean out those negative factors of guilt, resentment and inadequacy about yourself. Don't look for trouble or over react to situations. Just realize what you are doing with your moods and get rid of the limiting barriers you have established in your mirror.

Be able to raise your higher inner power and defeat those traits that apply to your central disposition and study from them. Because we still live in a world where we feel, see, hear and experience insecurity that produces trouble, be aware of all your surroundings. I'm not blaming the world for people's insecurities, but we all need to be attentive to the world we live in, the people we associate with and the lies people try to convince us to believe in. In order to pull away from affliction, each person must become aware and get rooted.

An imprisoned mind

Of course, we all know the world is only temporary. None of us is here forever; however, I'm sure many of us would like to believe that eternity is possible. But in reality, this world isn't real for any of us. The only reason we're here is to learn, grow and pass through, with or without being insecure. Where you go next is perhaps up to you. One thing I do realize is that our consciousness houses who we really are, and our bodies are a true reflection of our inner selves. If you knew that your conscious energy moves on to higher levels, how serious would you be about looking in the mirror? Would you try to create a new mirror and work toward a less pessimistic view of life? Various people imprison their minds without thinking of the consequences.

For instance, you ask a friend how he's doing, and he tells you every problem he has had in a month's time. He goes on and on in lifeless details to tell you at the end, "Life is hard," without ever realizing that he has entered a mental negative thought.

Each time you talk with this person, he's crabby, impatient or ill-tempered. When people spend much mental energy dwelling on the negatives of their lives, rather than the positives, their minds are limited. Because so many people are easily drawn into desolation, it is difficult for them to be watchful of imprisoning their minds.

But, if you could write "I am not a victim because I say I am not a victim" on a three-by-five-inch card and stick it on your mirror, most likely, you will stop being a victim of mental unevenness. I know that it can be tough to replace what you have become so accustomed to, which is a downbeat attachment to depressing thoughts. However, a person who doesn't work to over correct his or her mental state doesn't get well.

Keep an eye on your life

We all know that there are good and bad qualities within us, and we have traits that are both negative and positive that can produce negative reactions in others. Many of these traits can become excessively strong negatives if we are overly dishonest. This negativity can carry on back and forth if we're not cautious. As we look and pay special attention to our extreme behaviors that are sometimes offensive to others, we should maybe look at some of the reasons why.

An AIDS epidemic is spreading rapidly in the black community. Some people never saw or took the virus seriously and took chances with their lives. Instead of calming their bodies down, they kicked their bodies into overdrive and caught an illness. Others put their trust in hospitals that performed unsafe blood transfusions. Anyone who's ever been wedged in a major traffic jam almost certainly has seen the harmful side of many people's personalities, especially when it seems that everyone is in a hurry to go nowhere fast. Someone may be hanging on the horn or giving you the finger, not once realizing how inconsiderate he or she is or if the other person is having a serious problem.

All you have to do is watch television and you'll see clearly how the elderly are being taken advantage of financially. Utility companies and gasoline companies are charging outrageous prices. Credit card fraud, stolen identities, theft, scandals, sex offenders are commonplace actions among those who take advantage of other people. Most people are being deceived every day in numerous ways because of someone else's insecurity. Why? Because the wrongdoer is fearful of losing whatever he or she wants to gain.

During one of my breaks while writing this book, I flipped through the television channels to find the news and stopped on the court show *Judge Mathis*. A young man was suing an elderly guy for nonpayment of a $1,200 loan and for keeping the young man's valuables in his home. The young man claimed he had been living with this elderly man for two years and had loaned him money, expecting he would get it all back. It turned out that the elderly man was unable to repay the loan because he was using crack cocaine.

The elderly man was counter-suing, alleging that the plaintiff was behind on rent. I was dumbfounded at hearing a 74-year-old man admitting on national TV that he had been doing cocaine for two years because his body was sick, and the cocaine relieved the pain. I could not fathom how someone could apply such reasoning unless, I thought, the person was out of his mind as well as his body.

Many people are devising all kinds of excuses to justify what they're doing to themselves. Many people aren't coming up with the solutions for facing themselves without outside gratifications because they are afraid to face themselves. This is why the world is in the shape that it is.

Keep an eye on your life; don't believe that something is coming out of the sky to save you. Don't depend on false hopes.

Realize what you can change about your mirror and know when you are feeling uncomfortable about someone's trying to put his or her negative behaviors on you.

Heal the stress

Most people want to feel secure, but how can we, when we are only on this earth temporarily? In order to lend a helping hand to stop the confusion in the world, we must look into what is taking place in our lives first. Then we can begin to let go of our insecurities and learn to love ourselves as well as others.

To heal the stress, we must crush insecurity with sincere information that motivates and feels right to our soul. That teaches us how to do for ourselves and how to have self-control. And when the negatives come in our minds, we'll know how to draw from new ideas and concepts to reflect positive qualities that will contribute to building a new mirror picture. We'll know that condoms will not stop us from getting pregnant or contracting a sexual disease. We'll know that when we're sick, we don't have to desire unhealthy drugs because for every cause there's an effect. And we'll know to look deep within our soul and assist ourselves to overcome any anxieties, any fears or any challenges we have to get through.

And, yes, it is okay to change your way of thinking from time to time in order to concentrate on the positives. You may not realize this, but your ups and downs are part of your inner strengths to help you develop deeper courage and wisdom.

How much time does it take for people to come together and heal? My vision for humanity is that we stop waiting on disaster to happen before waiting to tell the truth; let's all present the facts and be honest with ourselves and others. Let's work together to throw away insecurity, lack of self-knowledge and uncontrolled self-discipline. Let's stop the nonsense and get back to where we first started: with love and nature. Put your trust in the source of truth. Lead your path in the direction of wisdom and give power to a self-reliant life.

SELF-RELIANCE

Self-reliance is trust in one's own efforts and abilities. With so much excess information available to better one's life, it seems as though we are walking around without even realizing what is really going on. This is an era when we can gain mass amounts of data to become aware of the world and ourselves, so why is it that many people avoid expanding their mental capabilities and becoming informed?

How well-informed are you?

In it's true essence, self-reliance requires confidence, and knowledge increases that confidence. You don't have to be one who overloads yourself with news, data and info. Be someone who has an active questioning mind, takes aim to increase your knowledge foundation and appreciates every element of facts that reflects its mirror to you.

You may find it demanding to understand what it is you need to know and are willing to try. But, if you are an individual who wants to know more and depend less on someone else, start now and pave the path toward independence.

When we totally depend on others, we give a part of ourselves away. For instance, we put our trust in large corporations to feed us their toxic products. We trust big authorities for their jobs, just to lay us off sooner or later. Instead of taking time out to develop our own gardens as an alternative, we eat unsafe food and are exposed to hazardous materials. Instead of being a driving force for our own self-made jobs, we work for others. As far as we know, dangerous bacteria could be planted in the food. We're not preparing the products so there is an open gap for suspicion. We allow the powers that be to pull the wool over our heads, and none of us hardly ever searches, reads, probes and challenges every part of the system.

Let's not get so contented. Let's get back to the basic rudiments, such as taking advantage of the sun's energy and growing our own fruits and vegetables. There are a number of options available for people who want to develop their own home gardens. You may not want to be dependent on one method alone, so you're going to have to think of ways to increase your knowledge and learn about alternative self-made energy techniques. I have a close friend who is always thinking and trying different ways to make his own lathes, tools and batteries. It is amazing to see how we can really take advantage of the natural resources available.

If you have land, you may be able to find some free source of power. Or you could put yourself out there and build your own solar heater and benefit from the sun's rays. If you are really serious about being self-reliant, you'll be amazed at what you can become skilled at. In order to be less dependent on others, *think for yourself.*

I often think about how many people are in debt and unable to work hard for the likelihood of their own self-regulating business. I think about how many people live in packed-together, busy neighborhoods. And, as a result, we sacrifice our lives in crowded bumpy roads, polluted air and loud noises and allow ourselves to sink deep into our reliance upon the system, which we do not comprehend or have power over. Consider this for a moment, the next time you make a decision, however small, think about its effect first and foremost.

Set your priorities
When you start to realize that your life is at stake, you will

stop placing emphasis on where it does not belong. You will begin to set your priorities on self-governing. I read an article on the Internet the other day that said as we become more self-reliant, we must explore the possibilities of living with less and learn to depend on ourselves for more. As I was reading the article, I realized that everything people think they need has been programmed in their minds by mass consumerism, greed and the dollar bill.

For instance, during each holiday, we spend money on every human we feel we owe a gift, and we spend far more than we have. We use excessive amounts of electricity, just to have a TV, a VCR or a stereo. It seems as if our main concern is to work at being successful; we work for bigger homes, and we wish for better cars. Why is this happening? Is it because some-one, somewhere, said we should, and we listened? Or is it that we allow others to thinks for us? Or could it be we don't know how to take charge?

Take back what is rightfully yours and seek knowledge as much as you can. Much information exists in small independent bookstores, in the library, on the Internet and in classrooms across America. There are no more excuses. All you have to do is get back to the basics and set your priorities toward living a self-directed life.

When we look outside ourselves for setting our own priorities, we are afraid to ascend. We are afraid because we go against our-selves, our inner voice, and we turn out to be compliant robots for others. We may allow this to happen because we allow others to walk all of over us, and some people do this deliberately to keep us down. But when things like this occur, you have to realize that these are lessons for your growth and progress. And, what you must find out is that you have to become skilled at fortifying your spirit and rising above obstruction. You may be in a situation that is out of order and out of your control.

Don't let it keep you down. Begin to set as many goals as you can and achieve them.

Writing this book was one of my autonomous goals; however, one of my biggest challenges was to refuse to be impaired by any crisis that tried to mask my natural abilities. Whenever I would give more power to my past mistakes or day-by-day distractions, I would block my plans to complete this book and would give way to my insecurities, which overpowered my confidence. But, when I kept doing my work as if I really enjoyed it, then I was willing to do more studying in order to complete my book project. I was willing because I know setting priorities opens the door to who I am and where I am going. I pushed myself to finish the book.

Have a sense of self-worth

As children, many of us never learned how to build up our inner self-worth because we were too busy being taught to feel validated in comparison to others, for being better than, smarter than, prettier than, richer than, more talented than, having better grades than, etc., etc. We have been trained in our childhood to look outside of who we are in order to define our self-worth. We compare ourselves to others without realizing our own self-esteem.

Many times, we aren't even aware that the first thing we do when meeting someone is ask, "What type of work do you do?" It seems as if businessmen are better than garbage men, police officers are better than security guards. We are quick to compare each other based on what we do and how much money, property and prestige we have. We do this without ever realizing that these things may make us feel better momentarily but they do not uphold us. We have to be internally driven by our own elevated sense of worth.

I find it very important in my interactions with others as well as in my writing to clear out any unproductive thoughts caused by low self-esteem such as comparing myself to others, feeling inadequate or being embarrassed by my sexual assault. Instead, I prefer to maintain a space that allows me to evolve positively.

We are here for only a short time, yet we don't even think about how many ways we can defeat low confidence. We waste precious energy on pettiness, meanness, heated discussions, stressed-out situations and drama to direct our lives. Since many of us have been exposed to years of distressful downpours, we tend to backpedal and walk a path of dishonesty, shamefulness, disrespect and trickery. The only thing we are quick to do is disregard our misery. But remember, the mirror will always show you, yourself.

We can say "the system" is the cause of our disturbing conditions. We can make all kinds of excuses about why our lives are a mess, but at some point, you have to wake up and realize that you can trust yourself and put your life back together. First, you have to be obliged, to look in the mirror and ask yourself some hard questions. Secondly, you must realize that the working of your mind is the power of opening the passageway to being self-reliant. All you have to do is believe in your own conception of yourself and become what it is that you wish to establish in your world.

When I was nineteen years old, I was raped. I think it must have been early morning on a Monday. Some guy came into my home while my mother and I were asleep. I believe a white towel covered his face. I was awakened by a rattling noise, and the rapist quickly pointed a knife in my face and told me to turn around. My discomfort caused me to move continuously. The rapist responded violently with the knife saying, "If you move again, I'm going to kill you, bitch!" My body went into total shock. Meanwhile, he continued to accomplish his main purpose, raping me.

I was panic-stricken. I thought my mother was dead. I also thought I was going to die until I heard my mother scream my name. The rapist stood from the bed and raced out of the room. The frightened young lady inside of me could not trust people or anything else again for a long time. Now I feel comfortable telling you this story. As a matter of fact, I shared this painful event with you because I have learned that regardless of what we go through, we have to be stronger than the experience.

I suffered tremendously within and continued to wallow in that mess for years. At one point, I didn't know what to do. My mother and I called the police the same day although the rapist warned me not to. And on top of that, I had to go to the hospital to get shots. The story of my rape was profiled in the *Chicago Defender* on the next day. I was stunned because now I was a statistic. I did not trust other people, and I did not trust myself for allowing it to happen. For the most part, I was losing my sense of self-assurance. I started being dishonest with others, and I became untrusting because I felt others weren't honest.

When you're in an environment where you're absorbing other people's energy, you are bound to attract who you are and what you are. Sometimes things happen just because you live in a bad environment. Sometimes things happen because you are at the wrong place at the wrong time.

I wondered why was I chosen to be a rape victim. What did I do to deserve it? Who was he? Would men like me in spite of what happened? Was this karma, or was I chosen to be a part of his pain? Many rape victims think illogically because they may not know what they're actually feeling. Most rape victims suffer from sex offenders' lack of self-respect. Some people have a high regard for humanity while others don't care what they do to humanity. The only way sex offenders can overcome doing damage to others is to change who they are: by being less attached to their physical impulses, by fine-tuning their minds and by seeking some sort of guidance to heal their deep hurt and pain.

I did not like being raped, but I did not allow it to keep me down for too long. Instead, I learned to channel the negative energy and direct it toward my goals and helping others.

Your past will always be a part of you. Why feel bad about it? Seek to live your life to the fullest, become skilled in your talents and refrain from making bad decisions that affect you as well as others. Study your mistakes and correct them. Teach others who are willing to change their conditions and have an ear to listen to support them make wiser decisions. This way we can create a better world for all of us.

Most of the time when others are sick, they need all the love they can get. Through seeking out counseling or positive mentors, perhaps rapists, murderers, abusers, emotionally and mentally depressed people can get well again. If each and every person could evaluate his or her intentions carefully before hurting someone, perhaps we could come together and recognize our worth as a whole.

Think about this. If you don't get totally undressed in your mirror, how will you realize your self-worth? When you are ready to take every piece of clothing off, stand up straight, look yourself totally in the mirror and say, "I will take back the goodness inside of me; I will be counted upon to do what is expected of me, I will seek a state of consciousness that will create a whole and pure state of living, and I will read, search and probe everything in order to gain knowledge of myself to release the impurities from my awareness." What you are affirming is that the road might be long, gusty, uneven and painful. Yet you are determined to release unresolved negative feelings and concerns, and mover to the other side of who you are to create a better person within your mirror image.

When you begin to allow your efforts and natural attributes to become a part of who you really are, endurance of self-reliance will radiate from you and shine brightly. Your determination for a strong positive attitude will overcome all negative forces within and all around you because you have accepted the truth of trusting you, an attribute that will endure forever.

CHAPTER 4

SELF-HATRED
VS.
SELF-LOVE

Waste not your love for hate.

SELF-HATRED

Self-hatred is a strong dislike or an ill will. As we live our lives to promote our dominance, possibilities and different values, we often attempt to destroy one another in the process. Because countless citizens misinform each other and give into their greed, selfishness and bigotry, we react with reckless and belligerent behaviors. Why is this? Is it because we try to disguise our own self-hatred? Given that there is a great deal of manipulation in the world, masses of people suffer from hatred through their own way of thinking, influence, fanaticism and subjection. We are like pawns in the game; we move around with a disposition of aversion just to get caught in someone's web or in our own.

Complex and confused

Today, men, and women, love to hate and hate to love. Because we are all born differently and with different states of mind, we often express hatred toward each other for being unlike. We often offend and abuse one another because we are dissimilar. We do this to try to dispel the inner tension from our own unpleasant thoughts. We don't want to admit to ourselves that we are all complex and confused. Perhaps that could mean many things to many people. Many people say they believe in and love Jesus, yet they kill and hate each other in his name. Some folks say they love children, yet they abuse them. How do we justify this mayhem when we live in a society that accepts hate as reasonable? We can't because we are defeated by our free will to exert our emotions however we like.

As you begin to witness how confused many of us are in this world, you'll begin to take notice of the self-hatred you may inflict on another. Whether it is for political rightness or different principles, for control or rebellion. Whatever it's for, you will detect that your behavior is a defense mechanism to cover up your own personal strain.

When you are ill and self-hatred has infected your being, your multifaceted conflicts are neglect, abuse and denial. You are trapped within your own weaknesses. Maybe you should look at your old childhood wounds and self-doubts to identify why you dislike yourself and others the way you do. By examining your pain, you can acknowledge and accept whatever is causing you problems. No one deserves to hate himself. But when you exercise hostility, you undervalue yourself and alienate others from you.

Although you may have rage against your family, friends or fellow brethren, don't let your agitated thoughts and inner issues bring you down. Accept your weak points and be okay within yourself. We all have winds of opinion concerning our diverse outlooks on life, but don't let anger or deceit define you. When you feel dejected, it doesn't mean you have to hate. Identify your feelings and find a solution to create harmony.

We are only bemused when we aren't responsible for our thoughts and actions. Learn to strategize resolutions in all your dealings. Approach conflict in a calm way. Talk through situations and gain perspective. Do you really observe your mirror? Do you observe the people around you who are showing you your mirror? I could not avoid what was destined to happen. It was impossible.

I greatly admired Leona, a longtime friend, as a human being I looked up to her like a sister. We traveled together, attended the same spiritual classes, talked about our future dreams and shared our most sacred secrets. That all ended when she caused me pain. I was sort of surprised about what she had done; then again, I expected it. When a person is hurting you, you have no indication that they're hurting inside. At least, at the time, I had no clue. I found out from all the people I introduced her to that she had been talking bad about me behind my back, telling private things that I had confided to her. The only thing I could think about was revenge. I wanted to kill her so I could release everything I was feeling. How could she do such a terrible thing to degrade me? How could she try to turn all of my friends and even my male companion against me?

These questions were running rampant in my mind, and that night the plot of getting her back was on. I was going to call her boyfriend and his mother. I knew his mother did not like her, and I knew her boyfriend was ready to leave her. I was going to give him the excuse he needed. I was going to spit out every single drop of negative information she had ever told me. Why? Leona was not the person I wanted to befriend any longer, and she deserved the same pain she gave me. Can you see that when you're not really looking in the mirror of you, you're bound to keep the cycle of self-hatred going? She was lucky that night because I could not reach her boyfriend or his mother.

I was confused. I wanted to call all my friends to tell them what that heifer had done to me, but no one answered the telephone. You know the drill. Most of the time when you're trying to get in contact with people, it's hard to reach them, especially when you're really in need of them.

I went into the bathroom to calm down. I looked in the mirror and saw how unpleasant I looked. The hurt, pain and rejection took a toll on me. Why me? What had I done? I cried, "Why is this happening?" The spiritual part of me wanted to surrender to love, but I couldn't. I didn't know how. Negative, thoughtless forces were taking over my being. I went back into the bedroom and sat by the telephone redialing numbers, hoping someone would answer. Finally, my friend Lisa answered the telephone. I started, "Girl, let me tell you what this so and so did to me!" You know she was listening intensely for some gossip. I explained to her what happened. She got all of the details and told me not to concern myself with distress. Lisa brushed the situation off quickly. She told me not to worry and started talking about her personal issues. Mine were suddenly unimportant to her. Before I could take a breath, we were arguing. I could not believe it. I told her that I did not have to take her mess and hung up the telephone. It seemed I was now angry at every living soul on the planet. I felt estranged, frightened and offended. I felt reckless, irresponsible and possessed. The whole world was against me.

When you keep the cycle of self-hatred going, you will attract any and every one, especially those people who are reflecting you. It doesn't matter who they are. People will show you how ugly you are. My mirror was negative and full of judgments. I didn't know then that Leona and Lisa were showing me how brutal I was feeling about myself. But, I finally realized that self-hatred was all inside of me. When I think back, I was addicted to conflict. For your own well-being, *do not become dependent on self-hatred.*

Have a natural remedy

When you're ill and your body is sick, it needs a natural remedy, the cure of self-love. The pain I was feeling from Leona and Lisa helped me to alter my mirror image. Although I had a strong dislike toward Leona, she and I came together to mend our deep wounds. In fact, my first remedy and valuable lesson was choosing better thoughts to improve my mental attitude. If we think with healthier thoughts, we will be much happier. If we think with hate in our hearts, we will be sickly. As long as we suppress our thoughts and emotions, we will always have to deal with emotional wounds that frighten us. But on some level we're going to have to reform our compulsive behaviors.

The key is to balance positive and negative thinking. When you are thinking negatively, feel it and completely absorb its energy. Then easily and effortlessly, be still, and put forth an image or thought that will uplift your consciousness to a higher positive frame of mind. That way you don't denied your negative thought, but simply feel its presence. You really do have to be the one who makes a conscious decision to achieve the awareness you yearn, the choice is yours to make. Because the mind is always seeking outward gratification and we sometimes weaken our bodies with our mental attitude, it is of major importance that we catch on to how we think. I found out the hard way that power of thought can take over our minds and bodies positively or negatively, but now I see that we have the ability to direct our will whichever way we like.

Let's fight to restore our mind every day!

Let's develop our mind in happiness by following a daily regimen of positive and beneficial thinking. It is titled "Love your whole being."

1. Love your whole being when you are feeling sad. But let no hatred or no material gains make you; it is only in your mind where you can control your actions.
2. Love your whole being when you have a strong dislike for someone or something. But seek to love everyone anyway.

3. Love your whole being when you are suppressing your emotions in useless behavior. But clear out your emotions every time you are aware.

4. Love your whole being if selfish people try to take advantage of you. But don't try to get even.

5. Love your whole being when you are confused. But don't try to confuse others.

6. Love your whole being when you might say I hate my mind, my body, my soul, my family members, my friends, my boss, my co-workers, my life and living. But love others and yourself anyway.

7. Love your whole being just because you are unafraid to live.

8. Love your whole being because you don't want to lose your soul.

9. Love your whole being because love kills hate.

If you don't want to become ill anymore, think on these things. Besides, how can you hate that which is part of you? We are all connected. Your time spent on hatred is a waste.

SELF-LOVE
Self-love is supreme. It is an inner peace of who we are and the truth of what we are. We have already mastered self-pity and self-hatred, how do we return to self-love?

Through Transformation
As we, slow down to return to self-love, we must first take notice of our empty space for inner peace. Many people say they want love, wealth and happiness; they want good health, strength and endurance, but it is amazing to find out that for many, no matter how

much we want, we never seem to be satisfied. We continuously go through life struggling hard trying to fulfill what true love is.

For instance, relationships are the most effective tools for transformation, but we often look at our companions as a far-fetched utopian love with an overdose of emotional attachments or heavy dependencies. If we feel the person is unable to meet our demanding needs, we go from one relationship to another attracting the same type of relations and situations into our lives. And, we tend to overlook that we are in relationships to help us grow. No matter what we obtain from our partners, whenever emotional concern arises from within, we forget who we really are. We forget to exist on a deeper, more meaningful level to clear out our empty space and get in touch with our inner peaceful self.

What we must learn to do is step back from our relationships, observe our love dealings for what they really are and gain a better perspective through true growth and being honest to say what we really feel in that present moment. Once you transform into a more authentic you, you will see that self-love comes from a sense of acknowledging your own conscious thoughts and working with them, and honoring yourself for developing wholeness and inner peace.

Although life is a process of inner alteration, we need to realize that we all have to work at something; that's the way of continued existence in the human race whether it's for endurance or strength, whether it's to heal our wounds or awaken our minds. But when we don't develop ourselves in relationships, we get stuck and hop around with many different people, which sometimes slips us into a depressing perspective. If we can't develop an authentic relationship, we rely on wealth and possessions to bring us happiness and we increase likings to keep up with identities outside of us, keeping us farther and farther away from our own genuine self. And as we struggle around trying to find peace, we can't because tangible things do not fill our void.

The more we shower ourselves with accumulation of objects, the more we subject ourselves to self-indulgence, which clearly clutters our thinking. We cannot see how to transform our self-pity until we stop.

Self-love is not about avoiding yourself by hiding in safe relationships or in possessions; it is appreciating that you can excavate inside the core of your living being and allow a relationship to bring up an existing emotional pain so you can heal. It is comprehending that your empty space is filled with temporary habits that you can have a handle on. When you are ready to step forward to pave the way for peace, true happiness and fulfillment through transformation of your mind, you will be able to gain inner perspective of who you really are and the truth of what you are.

Learn to dig deeper every day

Inner peace is within each one of us, but we must dig deeper in the time of pleasure and pain. It took me a long time to grasp that our pain is also our happiness. The more we build our ego, the more we give into exaggerated fantasies, eventually causing us to seek pleasure through addictions, obsessions and cravings. This type of behavior leads to false images of ourselves, and then we suffer in pain. For me, there have been many obstacles to overcome, many tender moments to mend and people whom I expected to care didn't. But I realize that my sole responsibility was to take things easy, depend less on vanity, depend less on outside influences and give meaning to my life by finding peace within.

When I think about self-love, I see magnificent beauty within each living soul, encompassing love for all. Life is about gaining wisdom, so when we turn inward and begin the journey to self-recovery, we dig deeper to find our pure essence. Has it ever crossed your mind that none of us is perfect? I once heard that advancing is perfection. Many of us want to be perfect. To me, that is perfect. The universe does not discriminate its energy to universal love, so why should we? The service of self-love is not difficult by any means. It is only by choice that we make it stiff. When you reach a final state of completion in self-love and view life in a generous, benevolent and patient way, you will see a beautiful reflection of you.

I would like for you to see how numbers play a significant role in our mirror image: numbers one through nine. Because every word and name vibrates to a number, representing the inner meaning of who we are, we create our realities based on thought through the different stages in our lives. Let's look and examine these numbers so that you can see the hidden power in your inner motivations and see how the root of numerology relates to the depth of your soul.

When you look in the mirror and notice that you are a pioneer, a leader or an independent soul, you are a number one person who strongly identifies with discovering your own abilities and who is always striking out alone and seeking experiences that will create your well-defined uniqueness. In the process of creating who you are, you ought to dig deeper within your being, pull out your full potential and take control of your choices. It doesn't matter where you are or what you've done. You must decide how you will use your creative energy to maintain your direction in life.

If you are a person who is changeable and flexible, you represent number two. When you're making decisions, you're seeking balance between two forces. Because your soul seeks to do most things in doubles, it is important that you aspire to bring harmony within your being. I mentioned earlier in the section on self-hatred how you battle with two opposing forces. You have to be obedient to yourself and supportive of others. Union is the goal of self-love, not separateness. Unity can only be accomplished through a meeting of the minds and compromise. Remember: looking within is the biggest challenge. Once you face yourself, everything else falls into alignment.

If you carry out the qualities of self-expression, self-love, the pure joy of living, you are a number three individual who moves through ideas and the written and vocal word. Your soul should be friendly, outgoing and communicative. The radiance and enthusiasm of your positive thoughts will draw others to you and will inspire them to expand and grow. Always remember when you go within, your creative imagination allows all things to be possible.

A four person is concerned with an established foundation, stability and order in all life forms. You should submit to your inner nature through building a strong foundation, working hard, taking risks and having order, endurance and discipline. You relate to earthly things like trees, flowers and beautiful fields. Dig loyalty, reliability and trustworthiness out of your nature.

A strong attitude of a five person is freedom of self-love, one always ready to take a chance. Don't be afraid to take chances because that is what we're here for, to meet many opportunities and various experiences. When you go within and feel an urge to go beyond your boundaries, you are filled with adventure. Seek to travel because you open yourself up to further forms of imaginative self-expression. You are curious, full of life and geared up. When you learn fresh information, your soul begins to change.

If you are a person who is connected to the inner harmony within you, you are a number six, kind and considerate of family life. This kind of self-love exists in love and compassion. Its longing brings harmony, truth, justice and sense of balance into its environment. Your companion, marriage, home, family and community prevail in harmony, truth, justice and balance when self-love emanates from you. These needs must be met where service and healing will begin to create better standards of living. Always look within for accord.

A seven number soul seeks to know the mystery behind life and its deeper meaning. These people are always researching, probing and inquiring about philosophical and metaphysical interests. They read lots of books. If you feel a connection to this number, begin by establishing more quiet time with yourself and asking yourself questions only you can answer. Keep to this routine of solitude daily and you will see that getting to know more of you is inspirational.

A strong, well-liked eight person loves to sell products and services, feeling affection for the material world. Because of their drive for ambition, eight people like to dress for success, wear expensive clothing and receive recognition and financial rewards. Prestige, expansion and growth are what eight number people seek. If you are an eight, you have the ability to overcome all obstacles and succeed through perseverance. With these traits, you will always be rewarded because responsibility and good judgment are ethical standards in self-love. Make sure you look within to bring out your power, which will give you peace if you help others in the process.

If you are a nine person, you are a coach, teacher, healer, sage or monk. When you dig in your inner soul, you will sense a joy that no matter what kind of hardship you face, you are able to lift your being as well as others. You have developed skills through experiences and tests and are now ready to share knowledge of love, compassion, patience and service to the world. Self-love of tolerance has given you this gift of life. Share it!

I wanted to use numbers so you could see how to broaden your perception of numerology. Besides by adding up your birth date, your name, your telephone numbers and addresses separately, you can determine which numbers represent where you are in your life. But remember your words, your telephone numbers and addresses change frequently. It would be up to you to study more about numbers so you can monitor where you are in life. Numerology offers an extra encouragement to assist you in designing a sparkling mirror image. When you're searching to dig deep within yourself, gaining more awareness can enhance and develop your brainpower.

Self-love will be a self-expression of who you are and what you must do. The selflessness, compassion, tolerance and service for yourself and others will be beyond what you thought you could attain. You will reach a total understanding and tolerance of others' views and prejudices. You will have acquired knowledge to share with the rest of the world. The joy of life and of being free has opened you up to inner peace because there is no end to self-love.

Tap incessantly into who you truly are. Divine potential is always waiting and ready. Gary Zukav's book *Soul Stories* states that you should possess the traits that attract you to others. All the love you could possibly want is right there inside of you. You don't need to fill an empty void through others because self-love is you.

CHAPTER 5

BLAME
VS.
SELF-RESPONSIBILITY

Your thoughts and actions are not someone's responsibility.

BLAME

Blame is to accuse, point the finger at or put the responsibility on someone or something. Who are we to blame for our cynical attitudes? Who are we to blame for the mixed messages in society? Should we blame our defense mechanisms or our parents? Should we blame our self-destructive manner or civilization? We all live in a crazy world, often unaware of our conditioned lives, often unaware that our narrow-mindedness and damaged attitudes are deep-rooted defenses we use to cover up who we are.

We live in a world where people do not want to listen or talk to each other about real issues that could make a difference in bettering our lives. Instead, we tend to send mixed messages to each other about our true feelings because we have a hard time identifying and discussing our emotions of dissension, hurt and pain. Quite often, it seems, we would rather point the finger at someone else instantly instead of acknowledging our own internal conflicts and unresolved issues. But to handle blame, we must acknowledge our feelings and communicate them without accusing someone else.

We all know that many of us, at times, are afraid to choose appropriate actions to eliminate blame, but to move deeper into a developed responsible person, we must recognize our weakness of finger pointing. If we don't, we allow blame to shield us, thus damaging us even more. When we disconnect our responsibility for each other and ourselves, we lack a sense of meaning and purpose.

Some people resist the urge to surrender their emotional and behavioral tendencies of blame so they can unfold and develop. All across the world, this type of defense behavior is happening in our families and in our relationships because we deny, reject and blame one another for our emotional deprivations. We prefer to pass on our problems, vindictiveness, disease and starvation from generation-to-generation because no one apparently wants to take the responsibility of resolving important issues: Like accepting that each human being is responsible for clearing out his or her own dysfunctional anger, fear, sadness, blame or other negative feelings. Like accepting that each of us ought to release emotions that no longer contribute to our growth and development. We need to become aware that learning to identify the truth of our feelings constructively does not make us abnormal or unintelligent. Sure we can reject or avoid our damaged feelings, but the danger is, we don't eliminate our self-destructive finger-pointing frame of mind, which creates fault-finding in others and ourselves. In order to feel empowered, some people try to blame others, but if you feed into their guilt about what they think or how they feel, you are feeding into their negative life force. Such an action can affect you if you allow it. To unfold who you are, acknowledge your own blame, acknowledge your own negativity and make another choice to carry out a healing path of development. That way you can open your heart to restoring the wholeness of your being.

If we don't deal with our true feelings in a positive way, we will continue to cover up who we are within and live life behind a shield because we don't want others to know about our hidden wounds or hidden agendas. More importantly, we do not respond easily and effortlessly to making abundant living our responsibility. Such action brings us to an even bigger standstill.

Why do we continue to cover up?

Some people cover up because of childhood experiences. Most parents are supposed to love their children and bring them up in a happy and clean environment. Most parents have done their best in raising their children, yet some parents may not have been emotionally attached enough to love their children because of other concerns in their lives. The children grow up feeling unloved because they sense an emotional disconnection from the parents and end up blaming the parents for not being there emotionally. This lack of love causes the children to feel desperate, confused, lonely and out of touch with themselves, and later in their adult lives, they resent their parents. Perhaps some people might have gone through this experience to some degree.

Because some people have never dealt with their childhood frustrations, they continue to cover up their damaged feelings later in their adult lives, which leads them into other big disappointments. For instance, we place high value on steady relationships and marriages, yet we blame each other when dissatisfaction arises. Many of us can remember how good the romance was at the beginning of a relationship, yet when the romance deteriorates, we slowly become involved in affairs or block out our unhappiness. Because some of us are emotionally distraught and cut off from who we really are, we wrestle through life blaming each other for our bitter defenses and misery.

I listen to people talk about their past experiences, and they are quick to tell you all about their pain and sorrow. But it's amazing that most people will cover up how they truly feel, put the blame on some else and focus more on their drama rather than on releasing their feelings in a positive way for a solution. In order for some people to hold a conversation, they must first tell you about their drama so you can feel sorry for them or live in their sorrow with them. Sometimes this is okay if you want to fall in their trap. On the other hand, many of us are gullible, and when we take in too much drivel, sometimes we can create defensive feelings in ourselves. That is why it is important to be careful what you allow to enter into your mirror.

Do you think anyone gets it? Do you anyone can change it? Until the pain hits harder, it might be too late. I have seen many folks suffer badly because they are used to the pain of blame.

My friend Joann called all the time to tell me about her boyfriend, who she knew was a cheater and a liar. She apparently didn't mind going to the emergency room to find out if she had another STD because she was always with him excusing his open sexual behavior with other women. All I heard was, "Girl, he's cheating on me. He went out of town again. He's paying this whore's rent." Of course this woman's favorite statement was, "Why don't he love me?" I could write a book on everything he's ever done to her. When you care about a friend and know she could do better, you get extremely frustrated when you see she doesn't want to change. You know men find her attractive. She could get any date she wants, and on top of that she has gifts, talents and skills, but she's waiting on this one man to tell her how ugly she is because showing her is not enough.

As the relationship went on, he began to treat her worse, but she liked it. He finally told her she was ugly. And guess what? She liked him more than before. Before she realized that he was gone, she was mentally, physically and financially doomed, all drained out. She called me more often to discuss her painful issues. When you have a girlfriend whom you care about, you should not be afraid to speak your mind. I asked her if she saw that the mirror was staring her right in the face? She replied, "No! I do not. He's to blame for how I feel, the condition I'm in; he made this happen. I let a lot of good men pass right by me because of him. I have no money because of him. I stopped giving my children the attention they needed because of him. I have no friends, and my family doesn't come around because of him. If it weren't for him, I would be doing a whole lot better." As I have said many times before, when your mirror is hazy, you can't conceive that *the mirror is you* and everything around you because you are clouded by what you think others have done to you.

I finally asked her, "Whom do you have?" She said, "No one!" I told her that she always had herself, and that's all that matters. She told me she hated herself, wanted to die and wanted to kill some people for mistreating her. No matter what I said, she could not be convinced that she was divine and that eventually everything would work out when she was ready to look in the mirror and not rely on someone to support her mentally, emotionally and physically.

Many people have this problem. That is why we must deeply acknowledge our own system of damaging defensives and begin to free ourselves of being victims, of blaming one another, of wallowing in self-pity and self-denial. We can offer ourselves much more than hopelessness. We can live life in joy.

Certainly blaming others is an excuse for not getting to know who you are. But you must take responsibility for your own actions and not allow anyone to disrupt your precious life. Use discretion in your relations with others and don't expect too much from people. When you have successfully learned from the past, let go. You are on earth to learn lessons for your growth and development, not to stay spellbound in blame.

There are no more excuses
After all, blame is a waste of energy. I hear a lot of my ethnic

folks say we get poor service, we don't get promotions, we sell out our people, we are disrespectful toward our own and we seem to be like every other culture besides our own. This is what I would like to voice to those of you who continue to blame others for your condition. Stop looking for other cultures to do things for you; do for yourself. Stop looking to be in the image of others; love yourself. Let's come together first, build our own communities, businesses and manufacturing companies and grow our own vegetables. Let's progress as a whole.

Needless to say, some individuals may find it hard to tether together and build. However, we must wake up and be willing to learn. Even though some cultures are biased and unfair to individuals, many people prefer to feel victimized in a personal way. Some people depend on other groups to do for them because they are so conditioned to their outlook of outside circumstances they get stuck in blaming. For instances no one owes you a livelihood, no one owes you contentment or pleasurable surroundings. To think that others owe you anything better than what you have within the depth of your soul is futile. How can you blame another for your conditions when you can do for yourself and change your mind-set and situation?

In general, you can't control what people do in society, but you can have power over your own emotions. Let's take your boss, for instance. This person has the authority to train you, promote you, increase your salary, tell you what is expected of you and hold you responsible for all duties. This same person also has the authority to tell you that you are no longer needed in the company. If you are generally a positive person, confident in your abilities and talents, what are you to do when you are let down and your sense of worth and well-being have just been challenged? Should you accuse, point the finger or put responsibility on this person? Should you become depressed, hurt, angry or frustrated?

We allow situations to devastate us when we blame others and ourselves. We allow blame to increase depression and feelings of low self-esteem when we don't admit that each and every one of us makes mistakes. We blame because we ignore and quiet our feelings about how afraid we are of what others think about us. If you look in the mirror and work hard to end your blame, you will see that people will not always be what you want them to be, people will not always agree with what you want them to agree with. Life will not always bend the way you would like for it to. Check your mirror and check it often so you can see without delay that every time you blame yourself or someone else, you make excuses to protect your emotional defenses.

The best way you can change the aspect of your blaming attitude would be in how you take action to make no more excuses for your unhappy actions and situations.

No one wins in the game of blame

Truthfully, you can really become an energetic person in determining the direction of your life. If you feel stuck in a bad marriage or a bad relationship or if you feel limited in your career, look at what you should attach to or should detach from. There are many of ways to shift your focus away from situations that make you feel inadequate, guilty and blameful. One way is by identifying the thoughts, beliefs and perceptions that keep you stuck in an unwholesome state of affairs. Another way is by willingly moving beyond self-imposed limitations and being straightforward in your relations with others. If your needs are unmet, it is your responsibility to be accountable for the choices you have made or are making. It is your responsibility to approach the person about your feelings, explain to him or her what you would like to change. If you are uncomfortable being around your loved ones, tell them. If your boss is paying you less than what you deserve, tell him, or make a decision and do for yourself. Many folks seem to think the world is the problem. How is that possible when the world is just the planet we live on?

We have to awaken, be less emotional and accept our own limitations without feeling the need to blame others. Our aches come from our own unworthy thoughts and unlovable feelings.

Think about this for a moment: We have politicians who respond to the needs of the public. They design the government, listen to our concerns, provide leadership and environments. We have the school board, administrators and teachers who are all responsible for the education of our children. The citizens of the world and the parents also have direct responsibility for the children. When children can't make a distinction between real-life situations and make-believe deceptions, then who are we to blame when things go wrong in our children's lives?

We all know without a doubt that everyone will quickly point the finger when things go wrong in our children's lives. The parent will blame the teachers. The teachers will blame the parents. The school board members will ignore the teachers' complaints. The administrators will blame the politicians. The politicians will blame the citizens, and the unresolved blame cycle will go on and on. But when the actions of those in authority are overlooked, the blame will go directly toward the parents for the action of their children. Why is that?

Perhaps no one wants to be responsible for his actions because it's easier to point the finger and say, "You did it, not me." When we blame, we hide solutions. Blame doesn't allow us to make better choices because it's easier to blame things on one person or on one thing. Why should we continue the blame game? What sense does it make?

The blame cycle can be broken if we alter our minds, come together and uplift one another. Remember this: Your needs, your wants, your pains and your actions are nothing more than spontaneous reactions to events happening around you. If you are challenging a negative decision that can be mentally, emotionally, physically and financially draining, don't be quiet about your defense feelings; acknowledge what is in your mind; analyze the situation and amend what you can before it becomes detrimental to you.

Each human being plays a role in this gigantic movie screen of life. Blaming others for the choices you make is often a dead end. When I was raped, the attacker was held accountable for raping me; nevertheless, if he had received some help before blaming his sorrows on me, there's a possibility I would not have been raped. The majority of the time when you're hurting others, you're blaming him or her for the pain you feel.

Yes, the rapist did a vicious thing when he demanded that I give up something so sacred. If this guy could have addressed his feelings, faults, failures and responsibilities before taking what I did not want to give him, maybe he would have thought a zillion times before blaming me or anyone else for his pain and suffering. Above that, he could have been in control of his emotions a lot better. Most people know what they're going to do before they do it. He did exactly what his intentions were to cover up his immoral defenses, control me and make me feel guilty for his afflictions. So putting the blame on others is only an excuse to justify your behavior.

Attackers who commit any type of crime are totally responsible for their own frustrations, insecurities and disruptive actions. They must learn to balance their physical urges and work hard to maintain a positive masculine nature and loving presence. Those closest to the survivor may blame himself for not being there, but whatever you did or did not do, you are not to blame yourself. Reassure, love and encourage those who have been sexually assaulted; tell them they are not to blame nor should they feel guilty about what happened.

No one wins in the game of blame. Some of us have admitted that we are part of the problem. Very few won't acknowledge how rude they can be. To understand people, you sometimes have to accept that a rude person is just that, a rude person. People are who they are whether they are blaming or being blamed. My concern is that a majority of us must get real and face reality. The reality isn't in debating about who's right or wrong, who's to blame or not to blame. The real truth is we need to look at ourselves, get honest and create some solutions for ourselves.

If you find yourself feeling angry or powerless, don't try to run away, indulge in self-pity or sit around thinking "this should not be happening to me." Face the truth of how you feel in a constructive manner and solve your situations in an appropriate, mature, coping way. Whatever your experiences are, you have to acknowledge what you feel; whatever is happening in your life right now is what you are supposed to learn. Learn your lessons and move on. But remind yourself to become aware of your thoughts and allow them to change naturally by feeding into more positive thoughts. All of this is a part of healing your mind and body on the deepest level. You must remember only one thing: As you learn to stop blaming others for your actions, you will become more in touch with that part of you that's the real mirror image you. You'll begin to experience life being less emotionally defensive because your thoughts are centered on getting rid of resentment and guilt.

Your soul has a rhythm—a rhythm of love. When your soul is not acting out its true loving and tender nature, you are out of alignment, but because you are one with the dynamic flow of divine vitality, let your soul's rhythm of love flow. Relax and freely let it go. When it needs a new surge of well-being, it will let you know. Stop fighting what you can't control and recover the source of your soul, mind and body. Blaming is old and out-dated. Use your past experiences as stepping-stones to higher elevations of self-responsibility. Deprogram old negative thinking and be about the solution, not the cover up. If certain things irritate you, release the frustration. It's useless. Look to the deeper person within you. I know it might be difficult to let go of blame defenses, but to keep your mind clear, active and creative, you must maintain healthy thoughts. Take charge of your infinite thoughts; you have every right to determine what you want or don't want in your thoughts, just as other folks have that right. So clear your mind and you will see that blaming is not worth mentioning. When you start with you, you can make a big difference because someone of importance is watching you— and all that can see.

SELF-RESPONSIBILITY

Self-responsibility is the ability to have full power over one's own choices and events happening in one's life. In spite of all the life-shifting frustrations and hardships that most people undergo, our primary goal every day should be to teach ourselves self-control, self-discipline and self-mastery. But first, in order for us to gain control over our lives, we would have to acknowledge that *we are our own responsibility.*

Let's look at the word responsibility. It does not mean to blame. It does not mean that you are wrong. It means one who is able to respond skillfully. If you know that something is not of your own fault but you are in a position or situation to do something about it, then you should look in the mirror and consider yourself responsible.

You have the ability to make better choices

Sometimes you can take a negative situation and make it positive by creating in your mind that you have the ability to see a better outcome. I love people because we see things differently in our own mirrors. I invited a couple of friends over for Thanksgiving. Later in the evening, I was thrilled to show them my artwork for the book cover. Needless to say, no one held back his or her feelings about the artwork. I was told that the picture looks like the devil. I was told that the lady looks sad. I was told she looks ugly. We are human, and we certainly can verbalize what we feel. If I had taken each comment and let it crack my soul, I would have been powerless to move forward and complete my book project. It is wonderful to listen to what others have to say, but what you do to defuse negative comments would be totally up to you.

I learned a universal lesson that day. It's okay to receive nonconstructive feedback because what people think in their mind is what they see in their mirror. Why get mad or lash out in a rude way when you know in your mind that trying to convince someone is a waste of energy? People see things in their own way just like you. Why should you do something that you might regret later when you can be in self-control and be responsible for your own actions? Don't allow people to move you; you have the ability to make better choices because you must have power over you. Keep your thoughts on the positives, and see negative suggestions as opportunities to help you grow.

The power is inside of you

Sometimes life's unanticipated events can be the greatest lessons to help you free yourself of self-pity and regain your power. If there is something inside of you shouting for transformation, perhaps establishing or completing a goal could make you feel better, facing your fears could empower you or ending a relationship could enhance your sense of power.

If people were really paying special attention to their intimate relationships, maybe they could realize that most of their problems arise when they're not being responsible, especially when many of us make unrealistic promises. Many folks stay in their relationships because of habit; some individuals stay because of their children, and most people have different reasons why they stay in relationships. People try to promise in their companionship that they will love each other for the rest of their lives. But what we fail to recognize is that love is a feeling that comes and goes or is feeble or physically powerful. How we feel at the time determines what we want in our relationship. There's nothing wrong with choosing to be in a relationship for a certain reason or wishing to be with another person for a lifetime; however, when we give fake promises of love, we set ourselves up for feeling emotionally powerless. Being responsible with your actions is not about impractical disguises, it is about taking your authentic power back when you feel you have lost it in a dead-end relationship.

Some folks try to impose their weaknesses on others so they won't feel alone. If you are feeling uncomfortable toward the person who is close to you, reveal openly to him or her what you are feeling or strengthen your companionship by not acting out thoughts of pretend feelings. It is okay to have a connection toward someone you love, yet still not act in any way that would cause you to disregard your power within you. What many individuals fail to realize is that we have to maintain our own individuality and get away from being addicted to another person for a sense of false self-assurance. Your happiness depends totally on you. When you are being responsible, you can expect others to be responsible when dealing with you.

Don't give anyone power to make you feel ashamed of yourself
Sometimes when we are careless in life, we have to accept whatever we've done or whatever we're going to do. That way

no one can hurt us. When I was in my early twenties, I loaned $300 to a guy I was dating. He promised to pay me back the following week. The four-year relationship was about over; we were outgrowing each other. In spite of this, we continued to need something to keep us holding on to each other. I realized the week had passed by quickly. When I asked him for the money, he said that he would write me a check. When I went to cash it, the teller told me that the account was closed. I was furious. When I got home from work, I called to confront him. He said he didn't have to explain anything to me and hung up the telephone. I called my sister, and we went to his house. His sister answered the door. We got into an argument, and she slammed the door in my face. In anger, I slashed all four of his tires. Two weeks later, I was arrested for criminal trespass. The following month when I went to court, I told his lawyer that I could file a warrant for his arrest for writing me a bad check. His lawyer spoke to him about it, and he agreed to drop the charges. So my case was dismissed.

Thinking back on that situation, I realize how foolish and irresponsible I was. I could have ended up dead, hurt or in jail. Everything happens for a reason. That experience taught me to take full responsibility for my actions and not be ashamed. I must admit my error and next time avoid unnecessary stress. It does not take a rocket scientist to figure out what is working for you or against you. Take control of your actions and think before you act. Don't give anyone power to make you feel ashamed of yourself. Give yourself a second chance in whatever you do and be self-supportive of your own actions. If you have caused a terrible situation in your experience, accept it as being your experience and reconstruct better situations through the power of your thoughts. Being responsible is in your consciousness, so manifest your responsibility by developing habits of wonderful ideas in times of adversity. You are talented and gifted. Why waste your dreams?

If I truly had known anything about self-discipline, I would not have gotten out of control and slashed my ex's tires. Was money that important for me to come outside myself? No it wasn't! The only power I had and still have is willpower—strength of mind to release the negative energy and dissolve hate. This is what self-responsibility is all about—*self-mastery*.

I was applying for a patient care assistant position. When the manager interviewed me, she told me I had something in my criminal background report. I was shocked! I asked if I could look at the report, and I was totally embarrassed to see the past arrest. I started to explain to her that I was in an abusive relationship and was not a criminal. I told her the case was dismissed and should have been removed from my record. She told me not to worry and that she would wait until I got my criminal record expunged.

This happened four years after the incident. I felt ashamed, like a failure, and wanted to blame my ex. Can you see how easily discreditable experiences can make you feel ashamed of yourself? That is why you must accept yourself for whatever you have done and be willing to take full responsibility for your actions and reactions.

Remember always to do what you can to make healthier choices

For the most part, you have to identify with who you really are to liberate what you will or will not do. If most individuals focused on leading healthier lives, they could improve the quality of making better choices. I sometimes watch the court shows, talk shows and dating shows and wonder when people will wake up to the fact that the solution to their problems is refining their sense of self. Each person must start with loving himself or herself. If we aren't honoring our lives or ourselves, it does not matter what choices we make. Until we start learning how to be sincere with ourselves, we do not have the aptitude to see clearly the direction in which we're traveling.

If you know having sex without a condom is to your disadvantage, why would you have unprotected sex? If you expect something to go wrong if you cheat on your partner, why would you cheat? If you know you will go to jail if you steal, why would do it? Isn't it true that what is done in the dark will soon come to light anyway? With choices come consequences. Before you do something, you usually know the consequences. For every cause there's an effect. No one but you can decide if your choices are worth paying the price for something you've done.

Are you going to be a victim by allowing others to make choices for you? Or are you going to wake up and commit to healthier choices?

I was reading an article on why men rape women and why some men like to kill. The article stated, "Because of man's jungle legacy of testosterone-induced aggression, emotions such as rage, jealousy, fear, lust, love, grief and gluttony inspire men to kill." It also stated that violence erupts because men do not understand themselves and that men did not invent rape; instead, they very "likely inherited rape behavior from an ape ancestral lineage." To me there are choices. Each of us has some type of genetic weakness, and we all are connected to the animal kingdom in some way. However, to say that men did not invent rape and very likely inherited it from an ape ancestral lineage is like saying people are not responsible for their actions. Because we all have inherited weaknesses, what reason do we really have that we can't control our hereditary actions of the choices we create? The system is set up for people to run rampant and make excuses for their irrational behaviors. As long as this is true, the system can and will benefit from people being out of control. Look at the growing number of jails, mental institutions, reality shows and court shows. Some individuals are making money off people who are reckless with their lives. Do you think people are going to stop their irresponsible behaviors? Well, I suppose changing people for the better depends on the system that determines what is moral or immoral based on what is needed at that time. But if you are aware or want to be aware, you aren't waiting on someone or something to help you change, you will know or seek to know how to be self-responsible. The mirror wants you to look; all you have to do is get started.

I realize that many things are bound to happen since people have all kinds of accidents beyond their control. But maybe if we listened to our intuition and used our insight to discern what we should do, we possibly could avoid some of our mishaps. Self-responsibility is a serious matter. We already know that people are manipulating each other. We already know that dishonest people do exist and that things are bound to happen because some people are irresponsible; however, that is not your problem. What you have to do is become responsible for your thoughts and control your life. The choice is what you make it. When you clear your mirror, you can't get caught in someone else's web!

You can clear a path to lead an honorable life by being persistent in self-control, self-discipline and self-mastery. As Les Brown says in his book *It's Not Over Until You Win!*, "Don't go where the path may lead, go where there is no path and leave a trail." If you don't, the game of life can throw you right off into someone else's way of life, and you might not be fond of what you see.

The only energy self-responsibility requires is freedom, equality, justice, growth, righteousness and choice. As long as we are accountable, we have full power over our choices and events happening in our lives.

CHAPTER 6

—⸎—

REGRET
VS.
GRATEFULNESS FOR LIFE

Regret not, for there are no warranties in life; the only sure thing in life is the potency of your soul.

REGRET

We wish things were better. We hope things will transcend. We sorrow over a thing that has happened or will happen; we remorse over things that have been done or left undone, and we weep over and over. Many people know there are no guarantees in life, yet we regret moving ahead for new things in our lives. We regret having an illness. We regret being in love with the wrong man or woman. The vast majority of people regret the things they have done and are disturbed by the things they did not do.

We all know that regret is nothing new. It is worldwide, and it goes beyond culture, gender, age, nationality, religion, social status and geographic location. As you move through life, you will experience loss, lacks and inadequacies. You will experience opportunities and tests. No one is perfect, and when things happen, we just have to prepare ourselves and move on. After you finish each day, be done with it. You have done the best you could for that day. Tomorrow is a new day; look forward to it and live your life to the fullest.

Move on

I have realized that regrets come from unfulfilled expectations of what we do or don't do. When we don't achieve at a certain level, we think we're lost because our expectations were unfulfilled. When a relationship goes sour, we say we lack the ability to move on. Josephine, a very close, life-long friend, lost her man and her job all around the same time. Ever since that point in her life, she hasn't been feeling good about herself. Whenever Josephine and I talk, she complains and degrades herself, not really understanding what's happening to her life. Josephine says she gave her ex-companion 110 percent of her precious soul, and she gave her job every bit of potential that she had to offer, but she can't quite figure out where she went wrong. Every time Josephine and I talk about her situation, the pain in her voice brings tears to my eyes. My tears are not because of what she's going through but how comfortable she is in her sorrow. One of the toughest decisions many people must make when faced with a sticky situation is letting something go in order to move on.

Take the time to think about her dilemma. If you lost your partner and job within a year, what would you do differently to make your situation better? Would you give up or take a new direction for growth?

So often, people get stuck and don't allow room for new growth. Some folks would rather linger in their past relationships and jobs because they're afraid to change or to take a chance. They don't realize that many opportunities pass them right by. I know that sometimes moving forward means giving up something we have come to feel comfortable with, and I know that life involves risk, but we should not be afraid to freely grow and blossom in ways beyond what we ever dreamed possible. No matter what life hands each of us, we can make room to fully comprehend the nature of change and expand our lives to experience each moment in a new way. But first we must make a conscious decision. Tomorrow isn't promised to any of us. The best we can do is move on and start fresh.

Although Josephine is in the process of healing her disappointments and inner wounds, her first step to move forward should be to accept and acknowledge her feelings. Instead of trying to block out what she feels in that moment, Josephine could make a conscious decision to recognize and develop other ideas and perspectives that will give her more expansive opportunities.

Lots of individuals tend to withdraw from anything that isn't certain, and things can be a little confusing, especially when our minds are cluttered with woulda, shoulda, coulda. However, the fact still remains that we are here and have to make the best of every moment and situation. I'm not saying don't take the time to be yourself or to reflect upon situations. All I'm saying is we tend to focus more on revisiting and reliving the loss, remorse and sorrow that cause us to continue to regret. We sort of act as though transformation is not supposed to take place in our lives. We forget that we can adjust regardless of what state of affairs we face.

Maintain your identity of how great you can be every day. Life will at times try to vex you and make you feel like you're not good enough. More often than not, you don't even realize that with the power of your thoughts, you can continue to stay in limbo. But learn to fully explore your feelings, thoughts and body; be clear about what you want, and strive to be the best person you can be. We are forever battling with expectations and situations we regret, but we never seem to regret our successes. What is the difference?

To gain knowledge on how to carry your losses the same way you carry your victories, you must study and recognize that your losses and victories both have value. The bottom line is you must accept that all experiences are nothing more than life changes.

Life should be lived, so move on and get started. You owe it to yourself.

Keep going and change

Life is constantly changing, and we are forever changing in its rhythm. If you find that you are still stuck in your unhappiness, don't worry, become aware of your thoughts. Change them and keep going anyway. Who you are is what you think of yourself. What you are is change, change to create what reality you want. If you are regretting anything, learn from it. If you are in sorrow, surrender to it and choose to change the sorrow as you move through it. If you are in grief, shift your emotions and allow love to come in, especially if you are grieving over a departed spirit. Your loved one may be trying to support you from the other side.

Many of our loved ones leave the planet unexpectedly, and it takes us by surprise. We want to believe that they are coming back, but they aren't. We want validation that we will see them again, but we don't know for sure. We want to know if they can hear us and see us. Many of us really want to know why people have to die. Because we don't have the answers, we grieve.

When it is that time, no one is ever ready. When it really hits homes, you're gone from here. I began to feel sorry for myself. I began to think about what I could have done differently. I began to regret just because I could. When it is time to flow with change, you have to roll with the punches and keep going. Our soul plan is forever reaching for the highest. Some stay here on earth. Some go in search of another world, and others go where they're supposed to, wherever it is. We weep only because we really, truly don't know what happens to us when it's our time to go.

Mo Money is a good friend. Some of her close friends call her Mo Money because she enjoys making more money. However, her soul does more than make money; her soul flies like a beautiful butterfly. When she walks in a room, you want to catch her and keep her for an eternity. When she speaks, you can feel the wind breeze through your soul. When she is upset, you don't know to what extreme. Everything she does is like a beautiful butterfly, beautiful but changeable. If you knew her, I'm sure you would agree.

Mo Money and I could always count on each other. We could forgive each other right away when we were upset. We could tell the truth about our pain. We could dream together and share our goals when we were being creative. We had a connection. We did not mask or limit the happiness or hurt we were both feeling about our life experiences. No matter what the day would bring, we could always count on each other for assistance.

I could feel some twists and turns about to take place in my life. I was despondent, irritable and weeping about what I had done, should have done or didn't do. I called Mo Money on the telephone one night to tell her that I was sick and tired of living where I was living. I told her too many of my so-called friends were driving me crazy, and my car had been broken into twice. I was suffering from migraine headaches every other day, having chest pains and a host of other personal problems. She shared her problems with me.

A couple of months passed before Mo Money and I talked again. When I moved out my apartment and in with a room-mate, of course, I had to call Mo Money to let her know that I moved. One day, I got a message from my roommate saying that Mo Money's friend had called. She needed me to call her back right away because something had happened to Mo Money. I called Mo Money instead of calling her friend. Mo Money's mother picked up the telephone and told me Mo Money died.

I was devastated, not believing what I just heard. Immediately, I went into the bedroom and started crying. I was regretting not being with her when she died. I was regretting not returning some of her calls a couple of months earlier when she was trying to reach me to discuss her personal life, as she had always done. I was regretting not telling her how much I loved her. When I called her sister a couple of days later, she told me everything that had happened. Mo Money had an allergic reaction after eating pasta cooked in peanut oil.

When death happens unexpectedly, many of us get totally confused. We don't want to keep moving. Some of us begin to feel uncertain about what we did or didn't do for the person who died. We begin to feel numb and lose our focus. We shut down in a state of shock, and the grief is so overpowering, we cannot see clearly. We feel as though life is a big dream that we need to be awakened from and that it doesn't make much sense at all.

If you are experiencing regret in any form, think about what Kahlil Gibran said in his book, *The Prophet*. "When you are sorrowful, look again in your heart and you shall see that in truth you are weeping for that which has been your delight." We have a tendency to forget that none of us are here forever. We get so complacent with our lives that we are only satisfied with being comfortable in our desires, whether those desires are people, places or things. But we must recognize that tomorrow isn't promised to any of us. That is why we must never take anyone or anything for granted. That is why we should not be overly trapped in worrying or desiring things too much. Each day is precious and fragile. Just think how your life can change swiftly.

If only each person would truly come to grips and accept that death is a process of a forever-changing cycle of life, maybe it wouldn't be so hard for one to stop regretting the past. Many of us weren't taught how to appreciate the cycle of death, but it is never too late to regain or revitalize your ability to find out how the process of life after death works.

My research on spiritual studies into the afterlife has taught me that human beings should try to spend less time regretting, mourning or weeping over our deceased loved ones because each soul that crosses over has the ability to contact its surviving loved ones. What makes it so tough for us to conceive this extra-special connection is that most of us are too out of tune with ourselves. We doubt our bond with all that exists. We feel more at ease with what is physical. We have allowed our strong remorseful and emotional grief to deplete our energy. And we have forgotten that to keep going and change, we stay with the process of life, which also includes death.

I know that life can be difficult at times, but no matter what life brings to you from moment to moment, honor what you feel and move on. The bottom line is this: *we must go on with our lives.*

You don't know what life can bring to you moment to moment

When I really begin to think about regretting, I realize how unimportant it is. If most people don't know what is going to happen in their lives from moment to moment, why do we waste time feeling sorry for ourselves? Is it because we are too attached to what is going on in our lives? Or is it because we haven't learned our innermost lessons?

When we are mindful of the moments in our lives, we honor what life brings to us whether it's calm or bumpy. Resmin is a kind, loving, thoughtful and strong spirit. He loves to create music, carve wood and design his own clothes. Resmin started hanging out with Darrin a friend from work. Darrin and his companion owned about three acres of land and invited Resmin and his girlfriend to visit. Resmin and his girlfriend had such a wonderful time, sharing their views, ideas and opinions, they visited Darrin and his companion more than once. Resmin thought that Darrin and his companion were really cool people.

One time, on the spur of the moment, Resmin needed to go out of town. He immediately called Darrin to see if Darrin would cover his delivery routes. Darrin said, "Sure, I'll cover your routes for you." While Resmin was out of town, however, he found out that Darrin never covered the routes. Darrin said that his companion was sick. Resmin was really upset—not because Darrin's companion was sick or because Darrin did not do the routes. Resmin was furious because he had given Darrin his telephone number just in case anything happened. That way Resmin could inform his boss ahead of time. Resmin started thinking about how much he regretted asking Darrin to cover his routes. Resmin immediately felt an aversion toward Darrin, complaining that Darrin had not kept his word and was disrespectful. "I'm glad I'm not like Darrin," Resmin said.

However, they were very much like each other. Each moment that Resmin and Darrin were in each other's company, they could not make out the reason why they met. Even though Resmin had enjoyed visiting Darrin, now there was conflict in the air.

When life brings you a moment of rough resistance, accept the transgression, no matter who you think is in the wrong. People come into your life to provide assistance in an area where you may be lacking and to support you in releasing unresolved emotional feelings or mental issues. If you are a person lacking in honesty, you will experience dishonesty from others. If you lack good intentions, you will attract nonconstructive attitudes toward you. Very often when two people are so much alike yet different, they cannot recognize that their painful experiences change their mirror.

In the case of Resmin and Darrin, their mirrors were fogged by negligent and poor judgment, which caused friction between them. For instances it was obvious that Darrin did not want to be totally honest with Resmin by calling him earlier so Resmin could call his boss. Instead, Darrin decided to deny his accountability. Darrin was not aware that his mirror was showing him how to be truthful and straightforward. Resmin found it difficult to accept that Darrin did not keep his word and was regretting that he ever asked Darrin to assist him. Instead of Resmin appreciating that Darrin was there to teach him how to be accountable, Resmin resisted the lesson. Unfortunately, when Resmin meets someone new, he often misses the lessons that person could give to make him stronger. But I am optimistic that in time, Resmin will identify his deepest feelings of regret, sorrow and bitterness and allow himself to release inner wounds that keep him and most us imprisoned.

When our mirrors are grimy, some people can't see their lessons because they're too busy regretting, blaming or neglecting their real inner feelings and life lessons. As long as you're living, there will always be moments when certain individuals will show up in your life to help you face your innermost uncertainties, whether it's through enjoyment or misery. Therefore, it is especially important to release and heal your negative ways and overburdened problems. Once you become aware that each one of us is here to assist each other to heal our fears, resentments and regrets, you will begin to draw healthier people and experiences to you.

If you are just getting to know someone, try to be honest about your feelings. Keep an honest communication going between the people you're relating to. Don't retaliate and say harsh words or create an unpleasant situation. Learn to work hard at getting some type of truthful feedback from your friendships but not to the point of physical attack. When you exchange your feelings with someone, one of the most precious gifts you have to offer each other is compassion. Be open with people; then, when life brings you a moment of laughter, your moments with be filled with love.

I know that we can get lost in our irregular behaviors and regret later what we have said or done. But what we must learn to do is overcome our foibles and identify with both our strengths and weaknesses. When you encounter others, you can appreciate their strengths and weaknesses because you can see the bigger picture of why you have crossed paths. Examine your mirror as often as you can. Then, when life brings you a bumpy or calm moment, you will know how to rebuild yourself.

Heal your mind

If you knew your consciousness had a combination of energy, vitality and creativity, plus a splendid comprehension gained through experience, would you still regret? If you knew your loved ones who have died were still here in a different form, would you still mourn? If you knew everything happens for a reason, would you still feel sorry for yourself and others?

Although regrets are normal reactions to grief, hurt and pain, you still have the ability to heal your mind. When we start to examine our inner realities, one of the first things we should do to heal our regrets is be willing to change our harmful thinking. Scores of us have been through painful conflicts, and many of us have the experiences embedded deep in our souls that won't ever be forgotten. But hanging on to experiences that no longer serve their purpose is a worry we allow to plague us. However, the purpose of healing our thoughts and feelings is for us to express all aspects of who we are in a loving and gentle way, and to share our love with others as well as get to the root of releasing anything that keeps us in a state of frustration or draws us into sorrow.

By learning to let go of thoughts and moods that don't push us to progress, we can heal our minds. Our realities can be bigger if we let new vibrant and healthier ideas uplift our mood. In the same way, life's regrets can be vehicles for recovering our essential nature. As we find ways of opening the path of joy, our new thoughts are our mirror shields. We will quickly begin to recognize how to overcome living in the past and get over old disorientated situations. We will begin to revive our spiritual self and consider making some of our dreams come true.

When you master your lessons, you recreate yourself. And

when you reconstruct yourself, you heal. If your family and friends see that you're becoming a better person, you can empower them to be better. Pass on what you know and teach others. Then they can take their techniques of attainable ideas to a higher level and teach others to pass it on. When we guide one another to heal and grow, there's no limit to how high we can go as a nation.

Most people don't even give themselves enough credit for the hard lessons they have learned in life, but they should. Once you are aware that all situations are for your growth and development, you are unafraid to unlock recurring regrets. Since we live in such a dense world, we must safeguard against being absorbed by sorrow and remorse in order to be effective in living life splendidly. Always remember when you heal your mind, you can achieve great inner drive through practice, patience and peace. I want to congratulate you for your long-suffering.

When you begin to start working on you, you will see that *the mirror is you*. Never forget: To uplift yourself from past regrets, you have to be sure to ask yourself these questions in the mirror as often as you can: How much weeping can I take? How long do I want to feel remorseful? What is good about mourning? How can I heal my sorrows? How can I prevent regretful thoughts from contaminating my future?

Trust your insight, be ready to listen and learn your lessons every day. Your future depends on you. Acceptance of all your experiences comes one day at a time. If you end up being miserable and regretting any of your experiences, remember that regret is what you chose.

BEING GRATEFUL FOR LIFE

In spite of the many sorrows that we encounter from time to time, there is still an abundance of things to be grateful for. As you learn to focus on the positives in your life, you will become aware that one of the many gifts each of us has is the power to express our gratitude. Gratitude is being thankful for everything in life. No matter what life brings to you, you can gather the strength to express appreciation.

If you woke up today with more health than sickness, be thankful. If you are aware that toil comes and goes, be appreciative. Quite often we are grateful for our joy, but when it comes to our unhappiness, we never seem to appreciate the complicated sweat. Many times, people fail to recognize that being grateful for life is all about learning and giving thanks for all things—life, persons, situations, belongings.

I hear people speak of not having enough, yet when they get an adequate amount of what they want, they're not satisfied. I have a friend who loves to shop every day. He's always buying something to bring him contentment. So one day I asked him, "Aren't you happy with what you have already." He said, "Yes, but I want more."

How often do you feel like you want more? I'm sure nearly everybody desires more. But, the truth is, if you are truly expecting to be grateful, don't think too much about what you don't have. Just cultivate the happiness of living, and you'll see how to appreciate what you have right now.

I'm not saying don't buy things that you like or enjoy. But we often take life for granted and get caught up in what we want without recognizing what we truly need. Material things are a good way to be happy, but true happiness comes from within and being and living in the present moment. Instead of juggling around in material comforts, consider seeing the loving essence in yourself and others. Instead of fretting about what you don't have, consider apologizing to someone whom you have had an argument with. It doesn't matter who's right or wrong. Being grateful for life is about spending less energy on material imitations and useless nonsense and finding the happiness to feed, water and nurture your soul.

If you can truly love yourself and others, the more love you will receive. If you can support and uplift others, you are blessed. If you are selfish or ungrateful, you must learn to recognize your worthiness. Since being grateful opens the door to knowing who you really are, anything you feel, wish or pray for is what you will attract. If you speak of not having enough, that is what you will find. When we ask for something in our lives, we need to remember to attract the highest good to develop our souls.

We constantly battle with the negative and positive forces within. Some days, our way of thinking can be quite tricky, especially when we don't focus on bringing out the good qualities inside us. Although adjusting to being positive is the way to think, every so often the difficulties of our lives can avert our minds, particularly, when we are faced with disappointments, poor health, breakups, layoffs and deaths. However, it is still possible to give thanks for one's troubles. It is easy to forget that when we lose sight of our positive essence, we turn away from our inner capabilities, and quite often, we can't see that being grateful is just a matter of perspective.

Your own inner abilities are what you make of them

When we allow the perception of negative thoughts to drain our aptitude, how can we appreciate our own inner positive abilities? Let me say this, until you are willing to do some deep inner work to build up your incredible power to improve your thoughts for the benefit of your own personal evolution, you may find yourself caught up in not appreciating all of who you are.

With so many distractions and unhelpful surroundings in the world, it is clear that many people are still in a moment-to-moment struggle within and don't know which way to

direct their lives. Many individuals are destroying themselves
by pretending to be someone or something they're not. Others
are avoiding situations they don't want to deal with because of
their own internal struggle. But these are issues we make for
ourselves. For the most part, tons of citizens are hurting each other
and don't even realize that infertile thoughts are the cause that lead
us into habits and behaviors that keep us feeling miserable or
unthankful for our lives.

One of the most imperative conscious exercises that we can
ever do for ourselves is forget about narrow-mindedness and
foreboding. We have to heal the negative attitudes, negative beliefs
and sense of separation that keep us victims of circumstances. If
not, our thoughts will create the inner capabilities of what we will
do. We must start to radiant a consciousness of abundance and
joyful living. We must start to develop an awareness of using
our mind to its fullest positive creative potential. Our inner
aptitudes are the doors to guiding a better life in accordance to
what we create. You may not know this yet, but sooner or later,
if you're open to cleaning your mirror, you will.

You can choose your direction in life. Learn not to get
trapped in day-to-day problems no matter what tough concerns
you come across or happy events you run into. You must be
willing to strengthen your dormant potential, dedicate your life
to true spiritual quality each day and help others establish a
spiritual life as well. An expression of gratitude is all it takes to
make a difference.

The key is to focus on your talents and gifts
I could tell you to think positively and your negative
thoughts will cease to exist, but it is not that easy. Although it
is possible not to allow a downbeat mind-set to control you, the
key mental factor in lessening cynical thoughts is to focus on
visualizing better conditions in your life, creating affirmations,

making bold declarations and honing your artistic power daily. That way if you are doing these things or something that you enjoy in life, you can avoid feeding your mind with nonconstructive messages, such as thinking that you are not good enough, that you do not have any gifts or that no one will appreciate your talent. Even if you have to push yourself to start a project, do so. Perhaps you may think this is easier said than done. But if you want to unleash your creativeness, you will need focus, effort and persistence.

Many days I wanted to scream and give up on writing this book, but my inner drive to study and bring out the best in me was my perseverance to keep going. I focused on visualizing my book, setting meaningful intentions and making bold declarations. Although the effort was quite challenging and painful, my appreciation and focus for this talent kept me stirring forward. If you are serious about bringing out the best in you no matter what may momentarily avert your mind or how small and unimportant things may seem, you will find a way to focus on something you really love doing.

As you begin to search deep within your soul to bring out your inner passion, you will begin to look at the brighter side of life as a spark of self-determination. You'll start to see that your fears, your worries and your distresses are all blessings to draw you near your hidden talents and gifts. You'll realize that the opportunities you often overlooked were expansion and progress for better ideas to come into your life. You'll see that love and joy, pleasure and pain, lessons and experiences, ideas and opportunities, talents and gifts are mirrors to appreciating life.

In opening the gateway to the inner self to express gratitude, each person has to see in his or her mind's eye that not only do talents and gifts take focus and effort but also our pleasures and pains with others and ourselves deserve attention. For example, if we are to be grateful for our pleasures, let's also be grateful for our pains. We say we love our family and friends, but when our love for them isn't going the way we would like, we love them enough to cause them pain. We say we feed our minds with knowledge, yet we are swift to include destructive stimuli to agitate it, causing pain. We know that it is necessary to take care of our bodies in order to remain healthy and energetic, but still we complain and gripe about our health although we abuse our bodies for the sake of pleasure. If we usually show lack of focus in our lives, we are subjected to pain although many individuals don't want to accept this fact. However, until one is ready to create balance in his or her life, that person will always struggle between pleasure and pain. While you're going through the process of clearing a fogged mirror, why don't you be thankful for everything and reflect on what you can improve each day?

Reflect and give thanks for everything

I would like for you to set aside five to fifteen minutes a day and write down things you are grateful for. Whatever it is, you can express gratitude. All you have to do is acknowledge your real feelings by writing them down. It does not matter if you are in pain or not. The process is quite easy. All you have to do is see yourself with new eyes. You can be creative when you express yourself. Perhaps you may want to write short stories in a thought-provoking journal, use color markers, colorful cardboard paper or pictures or draw one of your favorite images. Whatever you do, always keep in mind that you are grateful. Your project is a never-ending endeavor. Be creative with your list.

But before you get started, I want you to look in the mirror and say to yourself that you are thankful for all things. I find that when you affirm words into existence, you open the door to a deeper appreciation of all things. Let's take time out right now to reflect and appreciate the little things we take for granted—love, gifts, peace. Relax and enjoy your time to yourself. It's a blessing to be who you are. Besides, reflecting on what you feel helps to calm down your nerves and assist you to think more clearly.

At the end of this chapter, you can begin your list. Write down what you are grateful for. Your list will be an abundance of fun once you get started. Make sure you keep your list as a reminder of who you are and how grateful you are for all that you are. Remember, you can come to this chapter anytime you like. Most importantly, have fun.

_____

_____

_____

_____

_____

_____

_____

_____

_____

_____

_____

_____

_____

_____

_____

_____

_____

_____

_____

_____

_____

CHAPTER 7

FEAR
VS.
REAL

For the nature of fear is indeed instructed by the pressures of our emotions, mind and body.

FEAR

What is fear? Fear is a multitude of emotions caused by uneasiness, pain, fright and life's struggles. It is what the body dreads to feel or do. For the most part, many of us know that fear is one of the leading aspects of our existence. Our lives are profoundly shaped by the vulnerability of the unknown, which is one of the reasons we fear. Whether it is fear of learning new things, overcoming painful childhood experiences, approaching people and situations or facing life-threatening danger, fear is one of our most intense emotions.

In general terms, fear is the mind's and body's way of preventing and keeping away from pain and difficult physical changes. I have realized that all human beings have two choices concerning fear: we can either face our fears or run away from them. Even though fear is a strong emotion to overcome, it is part of our evolutionary life form. The strength and will of our fear are our tough challenges, concerns and burdens as mortals, but evolution has also made it our extraordinary power to succeed through areas in our lives.

By conquering our fears, we observe our human instincts. No matter how overwhelming or scary things may seem, as unique individuals, we have the power to master and transform our mental, emotional and physical well-being. The personal power we have within us is choice. We can take action over our lives or allow fear symptoms to take action for us. How deep are you willing to go within to conquer your own fears?

Occurrences are our instructions to move through our fears

In the process of struggling with fear, I recognize that all humans can gain strength when faced with fear. We have the ability to move through anything regardless of what the circumstances are and mold ourselves to become what we want. I know that may sound crazy to some of you, but it's true. No matter how mild or severe your fears, you can move through any pain, sorrow, emotional abandonment, criticism, financial hardship or human barriers. You can gain control over your thoughts and feelings and endow a strong courageous mind, body and life.

I once had a mental and physical breakdown. Suffering from stress, depression, anxiety and panic disorder, I didn't know what was happening to me at the time. I feared everything constantly. I feared not being good enough for my family, for others or for myself. I feared what others thought about me—if I spoke well, if I was smart enough, if my physical appearance was accepted. I feared that something bad was going to happen to me. My emotional and mental functioning consisted of a great deal of conflict and tension. Although I frequently interacted with others, I began to limit my activities. I felt more nervous, stressed out, afraid, depressed and anxious than ever before.

One Friday morning, I called my mother to tell her I was on my way to Chicago. I had taken all I could. My girlfriend had died in December. My companion didn't want to change his old habits. All of my so-called friends were disrespectful and full of problems. I told my mother that I wondered if I was losing my mind. Nevertheless, it took me twelve hours to drive to Chicago. When I arrived, I was tired and happy at the same time. My mother and sisters were happy to see me and I them. We didn't talk long because I was exhausted.

The next day we went to River Oaks Mall to do some Christmas shopping. We were walking in Sears laughing and joking with one another, discussing old issues. But little did I know there were some old neglected fears my family and I needed to face. My sister Celeste started out with her emotional hurt first. While we were shopping in Sears, Celeste told our mother that she felt deprived of certain things growing up. Our mother slowed down a little in the crowd, looked at Celeste and said, "I can't believe you feel that way. I believe I have done a great job providing for the three of you, none of you has ever been without." The conversation ended with my mother and sister arguing about how they did not agree with what the other had said. I don't know exactly everything that was being said because I was shopping. I just know our mother was upset.

By Christmas Day everything seemed to be okay until later that evening. I repeated what my oldest sister Darlene had said about our mother: she thought she knew everything. I repeated it to give me leverage and to mitigate the pain I was feeling because I was angry with our mother about a comment she made about my cooking skills. From this small confrontation, the both of us blew up and my sisters took her side in the conversation. I was stunned. My mother and sisters all pretty much came out and expressed what they thought about me. Secretly, I felt as though I was really losing control. I did not comprehend why all of this emotional tension was starting to take over my mind and body. Even though I listened to each one of them express their opinions about me, I was totally frightened—not because of them but because I was actually feeling as though a ton of bricks was sitting on back. I had no idea that my mother and sisters really wanted me to be the way they thought I should be.

I stayed in Chicago another day or two although I could not understand why I felt like my mother and sisters were against me. The day before leaving, I apologized to my mother and went to sleep early to prepare to drive back to Atlanta. I woke up early Tuesday morning, around four o'clock. I went in my mother's room to tell her goodbye. I felt as though I had done all the releasing I needed to do in Chicago. My family and I had relinquished our deep-rooted fears. My old friends were gone, and I did not have to worry about them. Now it was only me to face.

Driving down Highway 75 heading south, the moon appeared peculiar. I stopped in Tennessee because I was feeling mighty strange. My body had gotten extremely shaky. My energy was being drained from some intense pressure. I felt tired; my head was heavy; my hands were sweating; my heart was beating fast, and I could feel my body breaking down. I pulled over on the side of the road as cars were flying by. I was waving my hand hoping someone would stop. No one did. I began to get more nervous, so I tried to grab my cell phone out of my purse, but I couldn't, my hands were too shaky for me to do anything. My body went into shock, and I was afraid to move! All of a sudden, a clear, light voice in my head told me to move the car. I thought to myself "no way." Once again this voice said, "Move this car slowly and coast to the side of the emergency road." I started to drive the car slowly, about five to ten miles per hour. Before I got extremely nervous again, I saw an exit sign ahead. Now keep in mind that it was extremely dark. When I got to the exit sign, I was unsure which way to turn. Somehow I just turned left, totally out of control on what I was doing. I must say, when I got off on the exit, it had gotten darker, and I could barely see anything. When I made the left turn, I went up one block and saw a small convenience store on the right. I pulled into the store's parking lot.

At first I was afraid to get out, but I knew I was extremely weak and needed someone to help me. I got out of the car. My body felt really depleted. I went inside the store and asked the store clerk if I could use the telephone. She said, yes, with a curious look on her face. She handed me the telephone. I called my friend Nancy in Cartersville, Georgia, to let her know that something was wrong with me. The storeowner ended up calling an ambulance. The ambulance arrived within minutes. After running some tests, which came back normal, the paramedic volunteered to call a police officer to escort me to the state line. About fifteen minutes into the trip, I felt sick again and flashed my headlights for the officer to stop. He began to witness to me until a tow truck showed up and took me to Cartersville.

I wanted to know what was going on with me, so later that week, I went to the emergency room where I received a prescription for anxiety attacks. About three to four hours after taking two pills, I was worse. That night I decided to go to a Chinese herbal doctor whom I had visited before. I called him the next morning and made it to his office in about one hour. He explained that I had masked depression, poor circulation, a constrained liver, hormonal imbalances and inner fear that triggered the undue anxiety, causing the mental and physical breakdown. He told me ten things to do: let go of holding in resentments, live an orderly life-style, walk twenty minutes every day, participate in positive group activities, think positively, drink herbal tea, eat nutritional food, get an adequate amount of sleep, drink water to flush my system and be happier so I could heal. From that day forward, I did exactly what he requested.

Don't think it was all over; my body ached for eight months.
I had to let go of years of fears in a natural way; it took some
time. However, a very important mirror reflection for me was
learning that when you have thoughts of not feeling good
enough, life will always use others—family, friends, companions,
circumstances or occurrences—to show you how bad you feel
about yourself. My family and the nervous breakdown experience
helped me identify my own fear-based pattern of not feeling like
I was good enough. Since I was a teenager, I had always felt I
wasn't good enough for my family, although it wasn't their fault.
It was my turn to face up to those troubled thoughts I had formed
in my mirror. In fact, I needed to confront what I dreaded the
most—learning how to develop my inner strength.

Many events I had encountered seemed fearful at the time
but actually were not as adverse as I thought. I have learned that
we are the only ones who can make our lives better, exciting,
memorable and, most of all, learnable. We choose families,
situations and occurrences to help us move through our fears
and build our awareness about who we are. Sometimes our
experiences may be risky, destructive, stressful or uncomfortable,
but if we want to move through our fears, we must accept and
observe our occurrences effortlessly. But we also must be willing
to step out of old negative ways of doing and thinking.

Life will present whatever's necessary for you to bring out
silent suffering. Whether it's emotional fear of shyness,
embarrassment, rejection, jealousy, change or any physical
feared feeling, in order to overcome and release negative thinking
and unpleasant circumstances, you must be willing to deepen your
innate capacity to move through fears and understand that
irrational fears are only exaggerated by thoughts. Many times
we are afraid to change our fear-based thinking, but we must
learn to find the courage and strength to become fully alive.
Let your true nature guide the course of your life, and when

incidences come about, remember you can move through.

Most silent sufferers try to hide their contaminated pain

Heather was a good friend of mine who always tried to cover up her contaminated fears in jealousy. One day, Heather introduced me to one of her co-workers, Nina. Nina had just moved to Atlanta and was looking for a better paying job. Because I worked in the hospital and knew the human resources manager very well, I told Nina I could put in a good word for her. But in the meantime, Heather and Nina needed to rent a car to go out of town to pick up their belongings from two different states. Heather's possessions had been in storage in Ohio for some time, and since Nina was going to Mississippi to get her things, they planned a weekend trip. As soon as Heather and Nina returned, Heather called me on the telephone to let me know that she and Nina had an awful argument while they were traveling. Nina stopped by my apartment to tell her side of the story. They were fully in opposition and wanted me to get involved, but I took no sides; I just listened. However, because I had already passed on the word to the manager at the hospital about Nina, Nina qualified for a job when she returned. Heather was devastated when she found out Nina was working for the same company. I believe Heather felt as though I was on Nina's side, but I wasn't. Heather did not speak to me for two weeks. Eventually, Heather called to apologize for being selfish; Nina went on with her life.

This unpleasant incident illustrates how our negative attitude about ourselves is actually contaminated fears within us. To me, there was no obvious evidence or justification for Heather's being angry with me though she had the right to feel what she felt. It was apparent that Heather was already suffering silently with jealousy. Although she would have never admitted it, Heather's actions revealed her envy. Even though I was going through my own phobias at the time, there was something in that situation I was supposed to gain knowledge from. Later in life, I found out that I was a silent sufferer hiding behind my own contaminated fears as well.

Many times people try to draw back from their weaknesses in order to avoid the pain of facing up to a mirror that they may not be fond of. But in order to make our personalities better, we must explore our inner fears, ascend above our mental illnesses and take responsibility for our own attitudes. When you try to hide behind the face of fear, you increase your pain, and in turn, decrease the power of liberating your own feared feelings. Do all that you can do to reflect your own inner strength of healthier thoughts. If you see yourself as a self-conscious person, look in the mirror and tell yourself that you are brilliant, beautiful, talented and wonderful. A good positive attitude has much to do with overcoming and forgiving yourself for all those negative feelings.

Visualize an optimistic way of thinking

Sometimes in life you have to be ready to release harmful emotions and explore other options of doing what you have to do to defeat strong intense feelings of old negative fears and bad experiences. I will share with you one of my special work out exercises for getting back on track. On the first day of the full moon of each month, I write down everything I fear and want to release out of my life. It takes me about thirty to sixty minutes alone in the bedroom or bathroom. (You can choose whatever room is comfortable for you and stay there as long as you like.) I usually include a candle, a glass of water, incense and a plant in honor of the elements—fire, water, air, earth. The lit candle calms my nerves and gives me a feeling of warmth. The glass of water soaks up my swaying emotions. The incense cleanses my environment. And the plant represents what I am every day, herb in soil ready to grow and sprout toward the sun. I sit on the floor in a lotus position and proceed to calm my thoughts. Then I write down my fears on a piece of paper.

I go through this process for a simple reason: to unfetter my fears and express myself in a real way. (You can be more creative and visualize your own work-out exercise. I'm just putting some ideas in your mind's eye and sharing with you what works for me.) After I finish my list, I look over it in a loving, sincere, honest and peaceful way. Then I meditate and ask my ancestors and spiritual guides to assist me in liberating those not-getting-any-younger, contaminated images out of my mind. The next thing I do is fold my sheet or sheets of paper and burn them. The burning symbolizes that those fearful images are no longer useful; they cease to exist in my thoughts.

Because I know I'm working on changing for the better, I am determined to take steps and make progress to develop the skills necessary to rely on my own inner resources. Once again, I sit quietly and listen for my inner voice to guide me. For this to work, I have to know that it will. I have to keep an optimistic attitude. Fears can reappear day after day, month after month and year after year, and for me it had in the past. That is why one thing I will not do is play with visualizing or requesting anything that I cannot handle. Do not do this if it does not feel right to your soul. You have to find a plan that works for you.

If you are indeed serious about being optimistic, you must become aware of your fears and work to conquer them. Here's another exercise to try. Picture a bright rainbow color spectrum; visualize this rainbow as your protection at all times, particularly when you have fears. Give yourself some time to picture this beautiful image of wonderful colors; it will happen if you think it can. If fears try to creep in while picturing this image, I would like for you to know that fear cannot invade your state of mind without permission; therefore, raise your focus and try to picture the rainbow anyway. If that doesn't work, picture something good. Visualization comes from what you perceive. It is an exercise to help you focus in a positive way. There are many different ways to focus your thoughts and practice techniques that make you a more optimistic person. Keep in mind that thoughts and images are nothing but illusions. You can become familiar with what you choose. The power of thought is the strongest moving force in the universe: a gift that each of us can put into effect to enhance the truth of who we are. Now that you know a little about rising above your fears, there should be no more excuses about what you cannot do.

A constructive attitude can change your life forever

As long as you're human, you will always have expected or unexpected, major or minor challenges in your life to sometimes throw you off course. It could be a disturbance from your neighbor, a relationship break-up, a family confrontation, financial issues, traffic delays or any major inconveniences.

Randy had been an old friend of mine for quite some time. Two weeks before Thanksgiving, I asked him if he would help me drive to Cleveland, Ohio, on Thanksgiving so I could visit my family. Randy said he would love to go with me. I told him that I wanted to leave around 4:00 a.m. Thanksgiving Day. Randy said he would pick me up an hour ahead of time. When I called Randy on Wednesday night to confirm the time, he told me to be ready around 4:00 a.m. The next morning Randy never appeared nor called. I tried to call him about 5:00 a.m., but he didn't answer his telephone. At first I thought he was still sleep. Then I thought maybe there was an emergency. But as time went by, I realized that something was not quite right. I waited about six more hours, but still no response from Randy.

By this time, I was thinking that Randy should have called me at some point. I was furious and overly concerned about his well-being. I didn't know if he was in an urgent situation. I could feel the fear of anger, hurt and disappointment controlling my attitude. Part of me was afraid of what could have been happening to him and part of me wanted to curse him. But I realized that I needed to shake off my pain and bounce back into focusing on what I wanted to do. I called my mother to tell her I was going to make reservations for an airline ticket. I was on the plane by 1:30 that afternoon and in Cleveland about 4:30 p.m.

When you see yourself in a difficult situation, don't be afraid of the unexpected. It's not always clear why things happen the way they do or why some people do what they do. Usually, there is something for you to learn. You may not see the lesson right then and there, but if you're open to adjusting your attitude in a more beneficial way, you will. You never know; there may be a wonderful blessing in the air for you.

I'm glad that I went to Cleveland. I enjoyed being with my family the whole weekend. I was definitely surprised and grateful when my mother handed me a $500 check. Just think how easily I could have missed that piece of good fortune, especially if I would have allowed a negative attitude and a fear-based temper to get the best of me. When I finally got home later that week, Randy eventually called to explain why he didn't show up. He said he had no money and did not want to call because he felt embarrassed.

Looking back, I realize that sometimes other people's fears teach you how not to get so frustrated, stressed or burned out over large or small inconveniences. No matter what life hands you or whatever another person does to you, there is always a much more upbeat way to deal with life's challenges. And that way is by being responsible for your own attitude. At times, it is easy to get impatient, enraged, insecure or cynical and feed into these fearful thoughts; however, constructive thinking is the way out when you are faced with an unpreventable act of unexpected adversity.

If you change your perspective about any frustrating situation right away, there is a good chance that you will feel much better about your day. On top of that, there is a wonderful possibility that you'll recognize immediately that awful experiences are only unpleasant if you promote them to be. One of the most important lessons I learned when dealing with Randy was that a constructive attitude can change your life forever.

Do whatever it takes to convert fear into conscious mastery

Since fear seems to be one of the biggest challenges for many humans to overcome, it is important that those who suffer from fear work hard each day to instill an attitude of conscious mastery: the art of teaching one's mind tranquility and composure. As unique individuals, we can train and guide ourselves to overcome fears by not clinging to them. It does not matter if we are suffering from a stress disorder, panic disorder, depression, fear of death, injury, negative experience or severe phobia; we can refuse to give into despair and challenge life with willpower, courage, enthusiasm and drive.

In accepting this truth, we have the power to amend recurring fears, rigorously watch our thoughts through the exercise of will, focus and concentration, begin to manage your fears and find the right balance. Though a large number of people have endured pain in some way, conscious mastery can aid in balancing our emotional, irrational feelings and behaviors.

Here are five methods in developing self-mastery to get through phobias

1. Trust in your own inner awareness

Take the opportunity each day to put meaning into your life by practicing meditation, prayer, exercise or any form of concentration to reduce fear. Instead of being subjected to too much outer enticement, focus more on increasing your sense of well-being and creativity. This means you have the power to make subtle changes to resolve inner conflict. Choose something that works for you. The main goal here is to use your mind and nurture your soul. For me, every day I develop a habit of silence. Stillness gives me an inner peace that allows me to live a less complicated life. I know that I can't avoid all distasteful situations, but through calming my mind, I burn away fear and allow radiant energy to flow through my being. Some days, I feel a little irregular, but I make certain that I take some quiet time out anyway. If I don't, I won't feel alive.

2. Develop your own special self-knowledge

As we run around being fearful of life, working for others, keeping up with the latest trends, thinking negatively and living cluttered lives, how can we develop our own self-knowledge? One day, I was having a hard time deciding what I wanted to write about in this chapter. Then a very special friend sent me an e-mail message saying, "Sometimes you have to write about what you feel and what you know and combine the two and make one statement. Then, you'll notice that what you know to be factual and true is what you call creative and informative writing." When I read the message, I could see right away in my mirror the beautiful words Mr. C was conveying to me. I could see that I needed to build on my own inner knowledge and trust in my own abilities.

I discovered that all people can pull knowledge from the depth of their souls by identifying with their own outstanding wisdom. If you haven't noticed, information comes from the mind, whether it's your mind or another. If you're interested in utilizing your originality and paving the way for true happiness and fulfillment, just remember this—self-knowledge is the reality you create.

3. Stretch past your limitations and set goals

When I observe the world in my mirror mental picture, I view three groups of people: The ones who make things happen; the ones who watch things happen and the ones who say damn what happened. I'm certain some of you may see different groups in your mirrors, but which of those groups do you fit in?

The number one reason these groups exist is because some individuals are willing to set goals and stretch past their limitations while others are afraid to widen their confines because of fear of failure. But what many people don't realize is that we can't continue to float through life without purpose or responsibilities. We must push ourselves and evolve in greatness. Your limitations are your own imaginations. If you aren't afraid to set goals, why be afraid to stimulate your creativity and stretch your limits to make your dreams real. You are the only one who can decide how far you are willing to go to make your ambitions reality. Take all the chances you can and spread your wings.

4. Don't get upset too often

I read an article that said stress is one of the leading causes of psychological and emotional damage. I must admit, once again, that anguish is a form of fear. How many times have you gotten upset because of some ridiculous argument? How many times have you gotten upset because somebody cut you off in traffic? How many times have you gotten upset because of a situation you did not like? Yes, all people get upset, but how often do you?

There comes a time in life when everyone must decide if his or her life is worth risking for the sake of anger or saving for the benefit of love. If you don't decide where you are going with anger, anger will take you to a place you probably never want to be. So what is there to be upset about when self-mastery is about wisdom, patience and love.

5. Tune into your body

Many times, people tune into their bodies through drugs, alcohol, junk food, sugar, salt and other poisoning indulgences, but I'm not talking about tuning into your body that way. Instead, I'm talking about tuning into your body and bringing out the best you have within. What I mean is affirming your personal power from within by paying attention to your body through listening, learning, meditating, praying, laughing, being creative, and just doing something that aligns you with your body's positive force. If you know that your body is a temple in which the highest thoughts can dwell, I would like for you to look in the mirror each day and choose the most constructive thoughts to watch your power grow.

Here are four quick learning practices to help you tune into your body.

- Take time out each day and focus on your own health and happiness.
- Make positive affirmations every day that will allow you to release old fears that keep you inactive.
- Always remind yourself that whatever you want out of life, it is easily obtainable.
- Create and set some heartfelt intentions.

These simple techniques can help you develop self-mastery. I could continue, but inner methods are the basis for self-knowledge you can tap into. What I would like for you to do is extend your own explorations and learn that in order to become a master of your fears, you must unlearn old habits by training your body to clean out the old garbage. Your consciousness is an awareness that you can trigger anytime. You are the only one who can convert your fears and bring forth something that makes you happy.

Dedicate your time and energy to your motivations

When you have experienced enough pain, hurt and emotional

turmoil, there is going to be a time in life when you're going to say, "Forget this; I am tried of suffering." You are going to realize that all negative traits you have endured and all the situations that you were exposed to for many years can no longer be a part of your life. I don't care what kind of fear it is; when you are tired of chaos, you're going to know it. Though some of you may have already accepted your experiences and released them, some of you may still be in the process of disengaging yourself from habits of emotional and behavioral fear. But don't worry; you will breakthrough. Sometimes, you can't wait around for things to get better you just have to make things better. One way to get started is dedicating your time and energy to your higher calling. If you don't think that will work—do it anyway. In the process of focusing on your higher calling, you may occasionally be frustrated, distressed or even confused. But the only way you'll make it through is by continuing with your purpose in life.

All the fears that have crippled you in the past are just that—in the past. You don't have to keep wrapping yourself in the misery. In reflecting on those very trying times in your life, you may discover that your depressed fearful tendencies were passed on from your genetic connection with your parents and forefathers. Perhaps, you might have been exposed to someone's behavior, and you modeled your behavior after them. Or it could be that you have an unremitting view of negative situations happening in the world today. Whatever the case may be, when you don't truly dedicate your life to your purpose, how can you devote your life to security in momentary things, false impressions, misguided principles and other outside influences?

Many people fail to realize that fear will creep in even more when we place high value on things outside of ourselves. But the true solution in overcoming fear is in greeting a new you, planting new seeds of better thoughts, imaginative dreams, inventive ideas and ongoing endeavors. You may think that is easier said than done. Well, think about it; it is easier said and done when you think it can and know it will be. There's nothing to hurt you when your dreams are only images of what you create. When you look honestly in the mirror of the real you and take ownership of your thoughts, you'll begin to see what you are truly made of and what you really want out of life. Instead of concerning yourself with the process of habitual fears, worrying about outside situations that harm you or imagining the worst possible outcome in every situation, you'll feel a place of deeper inner trust, serenity and a consistent inner strength to practice a truth within yourself. The time and energy you'll have is the motivation to make your dreams reality. And, when you are in a zone of an endeavor, trust me, all of your ideas will be more important than fear.

Remember to take some time out every day and listen to nature—the nature of you. Whatever your fears contain, you can conquer them; just get busy. Once you overcome your fears, you will know what really works for you because you will shine through and devote your time to a higher cause. Let courage be your guide.

REAL

Being real is acknowledging the truth of your nature. Regardless of how you define your nature or how you may think of yourself, are you willing to know, admit and recognize the truth of who you really are? Perhaps you may or may not. The choice is yours. But the reality is this—people who cannot acknowledge the truth of who they are generally will portray fogged, smudged or shattered mirrors. Until you are ready to come clean and become familiar with the truth of your nature, you cannot know how to depend consistently on creating an exceptional selected mirror where you can see truth to power.

Throughout our lives, many people believe worldly illusions, desires, identifications, credentials, accumulations make them real, and most humans have been programmed to accept that these encumbrances are the way to an everlasting life. Because we live in a world that has taught us to lean on big business structures and worldly comforts as reality, the human mind translates the truth into wants and desires. All of these things become, after all, the mental realities and habits we carry in our own lives.

We do this to improve ourselves, but, in actuality, we aren't being honest with our real true essence. Instead, most human beings live a life programmed by many television commercials, advertisers and manufacturers that prey on our vulnerabilities and insecurities, which influences nearly everyone to look outside themselves, surrender to the manipulation of delusions and chase material objects to build up their self-esteem. If you believe that your self-worth is measured by the eyes of the outside world's vicious misconception, by all means, do not be ashamed to acknowledge it. In due course, everyone must unleash all fake images and reach beyond a continually hazy mirror.

In order to know who you are, you must be willing to move deep inside the core of your soul and fully experience all situations. No matter what dreams, schemes, struggles or tactics—you learn who you are through the formation of your own thoughts. If you are a person who appeases your ego through addictions of drugs, patterns of cruelty, deep sadness, temporary things or any similar obsessions, you have made that choice as an individual through your own mind, based on your reality. If you are a person who desires to be kind and caring, once again, you have made that decision by your own thoughts of what you choose for you. The thoughts we form and the choices we make reveal who we really are. Some of our choices are not always thoughtful or discourteous; however, when we truly recognize our own worthiness, our own power to expand beyond limits and the way to end a conditioned mind of false illusions, it is easier to break through the clouds in our own mind, expand our thoughts and draw upon the self-realization of the essence of our true self.

In other words, to truly know who you are, look further than the perceptions of the world and reach beyond all boundaries that keep the nature of your mind and body limited. Get closer to the realization of allowing your consciousness to be sacred and less wielding to the powers of the outer world, be transformed into a spiritually oriented person ready and willing to strengthen your higher state of consciousness; and more importantly, be patient and gentle with yourself. Even if your disposition is in artificial metaphor, be willing to give yourself a chance to reclaim your awareness by realizing that your inner self is the strength of real perceptible existence. You can still enjoy an outside life of external good forces, but give rise to deeper truths. You must find the best within yourself. You must understand that a medium that sends violence, a government system that sends lack of concern, a prison system that jails innocent people for greed and industries that release fatal toxins are not nearly as important as a life lived for a truthful purpose.

Work to recover your true self

Individuals must be willing to recover their true selves and do it in their own way. For me, reading books, studying, meditating and listening to quietness is my way to pull through misguided principles that are forced upon me through damage done in our society. Rather than give into viewing wretchedness of false power tormenting millions of people and myself, I prefer to strive to revitalize my nature through uplifting influences that fill my soul with authentic wisdom and love.

I realize that we can't look to the world to mend our nature.

Each human being must look into his or her own soul and open his or her flaws, shortcomings and make-believe mirror images and pass through his or her own test. No matter how often we implant fake breasts, hair or nails and undergo all kinds of superficial surgery, the image is not real. No matter how dysfunctional, unpleasant or tragic our lives might have been, the truth of our nature is not determined by unreal preoccupations that stand in the way of fundamental principles. Our true nature is acknowledging our balanced qualities, our creative energy, our extraordinary possibilities and responsibilities to others and ourselves so that each of us may create miracles in our lives. The more we become aware of our real existence, the more we can develop our minds and make steps toward self-awareness in the reality of spiritual genuineness.

When the human mind is in connection with its creative force, there is an inner radiant awakening for all people to reach, and that is to rely upon the highest human quality within your own consciousness. If recognized by the individual, one's consciousness becomes a power tool used to build up his or her own imperfections and shift into a renewed and transformed life; as well as a tool to lift up the human consciousness as a whole. What you do to improve you affects the whole human race.

Most people have spent enough time in unnecessary distorted impulses and false impersonations to attenuate their ego. Now it is time for people to know that petty disheartening fixations are less important than an individual with a noble heart. There are no possessions that can control a strongly held, spiritually renewed person, especially if the true self is repaired. However, inappropriate self-pride can come in a mirror image, perhaps keeping some people from full recovery. An individual who wishes to relegate his or her behavior in conceit cannot destroy false images, unless, of course, the individual chooses to recognize his or her shortcomings, begin to change unhelpful perspectives and live a truly spiritual life.

I have realized that when we are too excessive with worldly impressions, external desires and material accumulations, we seem to lose more power and self-control because the inner spiritual focus is easily distracted. We overlook the real mission of what we need to accomplish daily: reforming our consciousness about ourselves. In order to improve your human nature, you must re-create your own true self-image and shift away from fixed perceptions and their justifications. Begin to trust your innate essence. Bring to life ways to think and do for yourself. Admittedly, only a few of us know how to connect to our higher selves and become aware of the inner spiritual part of our authentic being without looking for an idol to come out of the sky. But it is time for all universal rainbow children to ascend and demonstrate love, peace, trust and harmony, take control over our own lives and learn to be responsible for what we do. When you are looking in the mirror of you, you have an option to mirror either a superficial self or a real soul. Which one do you want to recognize and improve the most? The source of your decision is within you. My wish is that you be clear about your choice.

Cancel out distractions

I once knew a lady who daily compared herself to models, actors, actresses, entertainers and fashion designers and tried to mimic their ways. Rosalyn felt as if being beautiful from the outside would find her a husband. She went through lots of men, never being satisfied. Although Rosalyn did date one man for several years, he turned out to be a fake, living a double life. Rosalyn was shocked when she found out that her companion was living with another woman.

What many people fail to realize is that you attract what's in your mind. Rosalyn felt that being more beautiful on the outside would bring her a loving husband. But little did she know, looks don't always get you what you want. Sometimes you have to get what you need in order to change your mirror. The mirror-image Rosalyn needed to change was her frame of mind and her false image about using her looks to get a man.

Rosalyn did not recognize until later that to find a husband you have to love your inner beauty first. Rosalyn also acknowledged that she no longer needed to compare herself to images that weren't her. Later that year, Rosalyn decided to do some deep inner self-improvement by finding alternative ways to bring out her own inner essence.

Keeping up with images that are not yours is a sure way to keep you distracted from being real with yourself. That is why it is so important to control certain outer forces. No matter what experiences you are going through, maintain your own identity in all situations or under adverse circumstances and honor yourself to a higher frame of everlasting reality through patience and diligence. Be cautious with your energy and guard yourself against being absorbed by pick-me-up and drop-me-back-down thought waves influenced by what you put in your mind.

When you begin to look in the mirror and concentrate on the real you, there is no way you can neglect the strength, power and depth of your soul because you have learned to accept all aspects of yourself, awaken to the place of genuine transformation and bring love into your mind, body and soul. You are aware that your purpose is bigger. Now all you have to do is plan and focus on something positive, unique and fun so you can bring true meaning to what you are directing your energies toward. Don't just sit around and allow physical things to breeze through you; you must be shrewd and have the courage to bring out an authentic power that's inside you. The more you look for effective truthfulness as a replacement for fictitious impressions, the higher your consciousness will go, and with determination and aptitude, the more productive you can be daily.

As you reconnect with your higher self, you will begin to attract conditions that are healthier for you. You will begin to associate with those who are perfecting their being and who are uplifting and encouraging. And you will make every effort to gather the courage you need to begin to disallow untrue impressions to affect you. The real truth of the matter is you have to make things happen for yourself and cancel out any distractions that try to drag, deceive or persuade you.

Reconnect with who you are and your purpose

As humans, we can uplift our minds and undo any weaknesses that lurk within. All we need to do is be patient with ourselves, acknowledge our motivations and reconnect to better thoughts, dreams and goals. But first we have to do away with selfishness and release fancies and ephemeral imaginings.

People who are willing to negate issues of life will begin to hunger for a real essential nature, not because they are forced to run away from external wants but because they are yearning for a new inner peace, a new purpose and a spiritual connection with themselves.

If you are interested in reconnecting the inner you, here are some real spiritual tips to uplift you. Take as much time as you need to reflect every day. Self-control is strength. When you can control the swinging pendulum of your mental wave patterns, you strengthen your soul. Positive thoughts are self-mastery. When you know that negative thoughts cannot rise higher than positive thoughts, you decrease thoughts that keep you weak. Calmness is power. Let nature calm your fire, and whatever you do, let your real soul purpose reflect what you're here for.

Here are some affirmations to remember. If you like, you can repeat them to yourself at least twice a day.

- I am governing the strong wind and turbulence of who I am.

- I am achieving all things through consecrated resolutions.
- I am balanced.
- I am willing not to create or be swayed by unnecessary situations.

If you find that you are in a weak state of mind at any time, you can exert positive affirmations whenever you feel the need by uplifting the strength of your own thoughts. All it takes is will, knowledge, determination, and focus. If you use this approach, you will be avowing your thoughts and maintaining clarity in your experiences.

I use positive affirmations to accept my authentic self, to create a healthier expression of who I am and to release imbalanced obstructions. Before this kind of thinking was imprinted in my mind, I lived in a make-believe world of false dreams and hopes haunted by my own descending thoughts. I was convinced that my weaknesses were not of my choice. I was persuaded by money, lust and outside powers that I thought mattered. I believed the reality of accomplishing my goals was impossible. The scope of my world was vanishing until I got tired of suffering and started to connect from within.

When you are worn-out and drained from your own discord as well as that of others, you must not seek things outside yourself, but rather connect to a greater inner embrace. That inner hug is embracing to know yourself by becoming aware of who you are. Embracing to see yourself by exploring your individual expression of life. Embracing to be yourself by accepting your authentic self. Begin to embrace every precious moment. Begin to cleanse your soul, make things happen to raise your thoughts and let the truth of your reality be shown through self-discipline, submission to nature, change, healthy eating, drinking plenty of water, exercising, thinking healthier, overcoming all negative forces and eliminating worldly possessions that keep you duty-bound.

In this critical time period of bringing awareness to your thoughts, you must also be aware of various egos who will try to take advantage of your weak spots, ready to swoop on any opportunity to see themselves as better or different or ready to treat you unfairly. Whatever the case may be, the opportunity you have is to embrace your truth and reject others' illusions. Some people may feel that they cannot avoid or find a way around charlatans, deceivers or false situations, but when we go through life without a bright mirror, it is much easier for us to be led astray by someone's path. And because of this, many people wait around for bad things to happen to them because they are programmed to believe that they are bad. Others are controlled by the intentions of someone else's thoughts because they don't know what to do with their own. Then many are absorbed by the influences of others because they don't know how to trust their own inner voice. To avoid unbeneficial comforts or connections with associates or so-called friends who delude you, you must not allow yourself to be programmed by useless and distracting influences.

You must develop ways to refuse to give in to others' fallacies, possessions, descending emotions and physical worldly attachments that make you ineffective in pursing higher trust in healing your thoughts and senses. You must also say to yourselves, as often as possible, that real consciousness is achieved only when your mind is no longer programmed by the activities of the comings and goings of this world. From now on, you will see a real being with strength. Your quest for the spiritual truth will come from a strong positive attitude and a purpose to let nothing get you down.

The higher you are consciously, the more real you are. The more you undo the mask, the further inside you get, and every situation will be more meaningful to you. You will become real by acknowledging the truth of who you really are. You will cross paths with people who can guide you, books that can help teach you, signs and symbols that will show you the realism in you. A whole new world will open up beyond your biggest dreams. The strength of your soul will be the real truth of your nature that connects you to an inner beauty, which will shine much longer than makeup, trendy clothes, money and other outside items. So acknowledge the beauty within your heart and bring out what is real about you. If you do, you'll be much happier, and your mirror will be much brighter.

CHAPTER 8

MENTAL BATTLE
VS.
BALANCING THE FORCES OF NATURE

The greatest battle to fight in life is the one within ourselves.

MENTAL BATTLE

Now that you know your thoughts determine your mirror, you must re-learn how to establish a mind of embodying thoughts of good, even if many of you may still be troubled, physically, emotionally and mentally. Nourishing wonderful thoughts opens your mind to a whole new meaning and creates love and peace within. For too long, we have allowed ourselves to be distorted, distracted and empty of our potential to be happy. What is vital right now in our lives is for us to realize a mental battle is going on inside of each one of us every day, a mental war. Mental is relating to the mind through its physical activities, its emotional responses and intellectual study. Battle is a waging war between two opposing forces: one negative and the other positive. This mental battle relates to us through the projection of our mind, whether it is an idea, a desire, a feeling or a physical activity. Whatever it may be, there is always a mental battle coming and going in our minds.

One side of us is full of confidence, spark and creative energy. The other side of us has a multitude of inner emotional conflicts of shame, fear, unhappiness and behaviors of judging others and ourselves. These two strong impulses are somewhat at odds with one another, which causes the war within. Though some people may appear emotionally self-sufficient, whenever the mind acquires a feel for a particular mood, it battles with likes and dislikes of emotional wounds, habits, desires or other life events.

By working on the mind and observing its inner course of action, one can become aware of how to gain balance and release the battle within. All it takes is a shift toward discarding thoughts that are against you, knowing yourself, controlling one's wants and behaviors, finding solutions to one's problems and training the mind to concentrate on love. The more we love, the less likely we will be at battle with ourselves and the more we become harmonious with life. Aren't you ready for a beautiful mirror? If so, you must dedicate yourself to purifying your mind.

Start taking responsibility for all of your actions and reactions in your mind

As we begin to study more about ourselves through our minds and feelings, something spectacular happens: we look within our own consciousness and begin to shape our thoughts, words, deeds and actions and take responsibility for them. Throughout our lives, most of us have been taught that every action brings about an equal and opposite reaction; whatever a person does will return to him, or whatever a person reaps, he must sows. How often do you take these statements seriously? Whether you decide to or not, that is the law of fate. What I have come to know is that those statements are true. Whatever a person is thinking in his mind, that is what his actions will mirror.

Many times, we are unaware of the internal struggle with

ourselves because we cannot perceive what will bring pain to the mind. Quite often, people are attracted to drama, aversion, afflictions and mental habits that aren't beneficial to a positive mind. Most individuals are so wrapped up in heated debates, flattery, backbiting, lying and fault finding in others, they cannot see that their negative motives and desires cause them to be at battle within themselves.

I can remember back in my unhappy days when I was in pain. Self-conscious and judgmental, I would lose much of my internal power by believing that others caused my weaknesses and flaws. Internally, I battled discordant thoughts of other people by making assumptions about their identity and judging their actions and behavior patterns. I thought doing so would make me more complete and confident; instead, I was supporting my negative qualities through my unhappiness about myself. Although I did not identify with what I was doing back in my impure days, I reacted in an arrogant and selfish way.

When our actions are not supportive of our well-being, we battle with ourselves. Our bad thoughts become a creation that we mirror in unhealthy habits. Part of our mind might have been poorly programmed early in our childhood, and we became victims of life through being pulled into negativity, ashamed of not being good enough, through concepts and beliefs that were imposed on us and through personal traumas. And our emotional wounds created discontented thoughts. But we must be willing to confront negative thoughts and release our mistakes and weaknesses rather than wallow in deep-rooted deceit.

We often hold others responsible for our frustrations because we habitually overlook the inner hostilities. And of our own free will, we allow forces to invade our minds because some of us let our senses get the best of us and prefer to hide our feelings in television shows that highlight hatred and violence. We tend to attract unwholesome acquaintances, terrible music and sex, all of which interfere with our ability to lessen the internal mental battle that is already going on.

Many of us are so preoccupied with unimportant and superficial matters that we are immobilized to look at what is really going on with our own minds. We abuse one another for material profits of deception. We embrace the image of other cultures instead of loving our own natural beauty. We are so caught up in the delicacies of the world that we do not even see the aggravation we feed our minds. I realize that some things are unavoidable; then again, we must control the things we do. If we're not on the lookout to care for our minds, then we need to ask ourselves who is. We say we want to be liberated, but we aren't free within ourselves. Instead, we cover up our vulnerabilities and weaknesses and hide them by clinging to petty motives

In order to end mental battles, people must see life as activities of thought waves that can be controlled by becoming aware and taking responsibility for their own minds. They must establish a much higher purpose to nurture and develop a quest for goodness and love, expressed through spiritual practices, prayer and mediation. Once that has been accomplished, the only real strengthening work required is effort, dedication, discipline and continuous transformation. Each day can be focused positively on utilizing all your energy to uplift your soul by concentrating on clearer ideas and higher thoughts to break habit-forming destructive circumstances and experiences, thus, allowing you to overcome obstacles and refrain from confusion. When you learn to focus and concentrate more on your skills, you have the power to truthfully transform yourself, as well as utilize your honed skills to provide a sense of service to others. And you'll start in on a more beautiful mirror through pure love and peace.

Start being more loving

Each day should be a day when you love yourself and have positive and loving interactions with others. The more you love, the less emotionally involved you are in war with yourself or another. You do not have to cover up anymore in dramatic portrayals. You can merely free negative qualities within and gain the aptitude to connect with wholesome love inside to reflect the goodness of you. In time, you will see yourself a master of your moods, and all types of positive brightness will appear in your mirror. The only setback now would be if you don't carry out the changes in you to make your mirror well again. That's only if your mirror is hazy or requires clarity.

A couple of my friends have said to me, "I love him, but I'm not in love with him." What is the difference? When I first heard the statement, I was completely baffled. Some people mentally battle with whether they love a person. How can we love another or ourselves when we put limitations on love? Love is not something you add to or take away from when you get tired of it. Love is Love. Love is encompassing of all things. How can you say you love this person, but you're not in love? Could it be that the love you're looking for is lust after your desires? Only you know what kind of love you're wanting. Just be prepared for the kind of love you say you may want or don't want, or better yet, don't have. To me, love is pure peace—accepting all people, situations, circumstances and things as they are and making them better. It is okay to be in love, but it is more important to be a loving person.

Mental battles aren't hard to let go if you can renounce unhelpful thoughts and bad habits. If you are troubled physically, emotionally and mentally, there is only one way you can free yourself from emotional responses that are useless—ideas, greediness, selfishness, jealousy—and end physical activities that place you in adverse company with others. You can find relief through an uncontaminated consciousness, non-attachment to things, eradication of poignant reactions to circumstances and people and the help of the Co-Creator—yourself.

I want you to surround yourself with loving people who love themselves and honor society. Become active within a community that serves others and make yourself aware of available resources that contribute to society. When you do, you won't have time to combat with yourself because you are using your thoughts for higher vibrations of positive strength. What you must remember is that a loving person cannot occupy a mind of love and war at the same. Either you are going to live in this world on a lower mental state and battle with yourself or you're going to concentrate on love and sharing it with others.

We know now that many of us are affected by influence in some way or another, by our environment or by delusions of the world. However, what will you use your mind for? Will it be your mental battles or your skills to overpower them? The answer is for you!

Janet is an older woman I know. When we communicate, she's always on a positive, harmonic rhythm. I have never noticed a negative gesture from her, nor have I ever had a negative encounter with her. She's a walking, talking and doing divine woman. She loves to read books that are inspirational, thought provoking and informative for her growth and development. She loves every form of artwork. She loves healthy food, plenty of water, fresh air, beautiful natural surroundings and people.

In the short time I've known her, I have learned how to be more of a divine soul. When she told me a little about her life, I was surprised by her story. She was born in poverty and had a mental deficiency. As a child, she had to attend a special school for the mentally retarded. Janet could not speak English very well when she was younger. She was teased by her peers and conformed to unhealthy conditions in her environment. She was lost and confused for many years. Janet didn't know how to stop her mental afflictions until she was old enough to release her emotional wounds and heal her mind. She said years passed before she started to conceive of her mental condition. Her disorder and instability pushed her to utilize her spare time to develop her dormant powers. The visions from her thoughts expanded her mind to see a larger capacity of a better life ahead. It wasn't long before her mental battle was out of harmony with her old mentality.

The forces of her mental strength can now master the growth and opportunities that fit the compass of her expanding powers. Janet said, "I was born in poverty and had a mental deficiency because I lacked the lessons from my past lives. When I decided to hold the force within, the storms eased." She also conveyed to me that she was accountable for every action and reaction of her mental powers. Her last words to me before she left that night were "you must have self-discipline and a mental outlet to channel both positive and negative forces into enriching deeds because the highest vision of love urges you into action, and most importantly, your own thoughts to exercise the will of the Creator and witness all that you take in, radiantly."

I was astounded. Her purity was something you would want for all humanity. Her to-the-point story changed my life. Janet currently helps others mend their lives. When you are in a mental battle with yourself, all you need to do is gravitate to your ideal and become the master of your thoughts. Think about Janet's story and realize that you, too, can break the barriers and rise. Your greatest achievements can be the beauty that forms in your mind, the purest thoughts that nourish your soul and a being who is always loving. How are you going to grip your flame? The torch is the apple of your true essence. Rise and evolve past the war and balance the forces of nature that are you.

BALANCING THE FORCES OF NATURE

I really do envision that you have come close to seeing a mirror of great health, joy and happiness. Nowadays, some people feel determined to make their lives more content. Others merely give up and try to run away from their challenges in life. But the strongest, brightest and healthiest way to move through life is by balancing the forces of nature, becoming aware of yourself through harmonizing the inside of your body, mind and soul.

As human beings, we have forgotten that one of the most effective tools for creating balance in our lives is developing our consciousness to create or change forms and conditions through the power of our thoughts.

Because we have succumbed to releasing negative energy into our minds and refusing to let go of the fast-paced world, many of us are not conscious of monitoring our thoughts, words and actions to make time for balancing our lives to relieve pressure. With family members needing our time, bills cluttering the kitchen table, household tasks needing to be done and employers breaking our bodies, we don't move forward to support our growth and well-being, especially when we're aggravated with life's situations and unexpected struggles. However, we must look within ourselves and depend on our own omnipresence. All we need to do is become reconnected to our own higher spiritual consciousness so we can uplift our thoughts, change our unbalanced conditions through the power of our thoughts and begin to take the next appropriate step to balance our lives and sustain greater joy, peace and harmony. The key is to use the most effective tool or technique to uplift your thoughts.

There are three basic universal laws that I utilize. One is called the law of mind action, which means, "whatever we hold in our mind, will be pictured in our lives." Another law is the law of cause and effect. This means that "every experience that manifests at the physical level, is the effect of a cause produced at the mental, emotional or spiritual level." Finally, there is the law of correspondence. This law states that "what you draw to you is what you are." These are useful tools to remind you, if you're open, that you have the power to change any condition or situation to correct any habit, behavior, feeling or thought that hinders your highest good. You can do further research into the studies of universal laws and principles by taking metaphysics, or attending a spiritual workshop that offers the awareness of spiritual laws, principles and tools to support you in being balanced.

When we move into action to enhance our consciousness and establish a spiritual life as top priority, we begin to pay special attention to our body's spiritual, emotional, mental and physical needs that requires balancing. We find ways to heal all aspects of our emotional, mental and physical elements because our true nature is clearing the path of all blockages and barriers. We begin to depend on our own innate wisdom, and we start to focus on something constructive. We begin to set priorities, accomplish goals and reflect upon a regular self-nurturing state of existence.

Writing this book has not been effortless. In fact, it has helped me to do some self-healing in learning ways to balance my life. I know I must remember to meditate, create positive affirmations, take some time out to pamper myself, share love with my partner, family and friends, prioritize my goals, acknowledge my spiritual and emotional needs and explore ways to fulfill myself in life. For years, I was subjugated by ignorance, misunderstanding and remission because I was short of maintaining a balance in every aspect of my existence. I neglected my craft and artistic ways because I allowed my negative thinking to decrease my energy flow and the external light of material things to create an unstable foundation for me. My mirror image was distorted, but I learned a valuable lesson throughout this whole ordeal of unevenness. I learned that whatever situation I am in, I must first build a strong foundation for storing goodness within my soul, open a channel for effective conscious thinking that supports an attitude of truthfulness and an inner quality that pulls forward staying balanced on a regular basis.

For those of you who have wasted your energies in negative emotions and in unhappiness, now is the time to burn out those emotional hurts and mental wounds and begin to position yourself through restoring your consciousness to create or change forms and conditions through the power of your thoughts. You can begin right now and build a balanced healthy, happy body and soul.

Store goodness in your soul by taking care of yourself

Most people, whether male or female, have a tendency to chain themselves to their weaknesses rather than taking care of themselves and their imperfections. Too often, people store themselves up with so many different ineffective misconceptions, ideas and habits that they become servants to false mirror pictures of themselves, indicating an imbalance in nature. Their inner world of negative thoughts begins to shape their outer world of very bad circumstances. Their lives become blurred because they deny their good, have unclear principles and are unwilling to fight earthly temptations.

If you have formed a weakness that persistently slows down your physical, emotional, mental and spiritual body, allow me to share with you what it takes to store goodness in your soul. For one, you have to take the first step to identify what your weaknesses are. Then you have to be willing to see the loving essence within yourself to move beyond any discomfort, fear, judgments or behavior patterns that create negative emotional and mental stagnation. If something within you is creating continuous conflict, the fight or weakness is not with people or the world, but it is within you. To restore your mental, physical or emotional deficiencies and balance them, you must make your thoughts and acts constructive. You must learn to sustain a clear and smooth pattern of good thinking and keep appreciating and honoring yourself.

Quite often, we forget that the smallest negative thought pollutes our consciousness and too much of anything can cause us to strive constantly for attention in unhealthy ways, which keeps us unbalanced. So having to worry about finances, jobs, relationships or control over someone's life becomes unimportant, especially when we're feeling out of touch with ourselves. If we are to work in harmony with every aspect of our being, we must begin to tap into the darkness of our soul and dominate the positive part to bring out the good and create perfect balance. We have wasted enough of our life energies in the light of outside indulgences. Now it is time to give our power to the areas within and take control over our lives.

But the first thing I would like for you to do is commit to your own inner good, commit to yielding a virtuous life and maintain that good flow. When you're on a righteous path and aspire to remain righteous, you have certain obligations. You are required to aim your existence on the sun, where you can warm your spirit, soul, mind and body to heal, radiate love and nourish all that you are by nature. You are required to associate with the feminine and masculine part of you, which is creative energy and active will power to unblock your imbalances.

Almost every month, I visit the same Chinese doctor. Each time we talk, he tells me how important it is to warm, center and strengthen my energy. He says one should significantly know about the two life forces: the feminine and masculine energies that are the general characteristics associated with the light and darkness of their living form. He says in order to have a flow of energy that is clear and balanced, one should make every effort to align his or her female and male energy with persistence to make well any kind of deficiency within. I honestly want you to find out with your mind's eye just how light and darkness work. Let's use the symbols of the nine charkas of the body.

Chakras are wheels, the spinning vortexes of energy. They are centers of force located within our etheric body through which we receive, transmit and process life energies. Each chakra is a central point of life force connecting to spirit, soul, mind and body. These chakras are the body's nine energy centers that work to balance our lives every single day. On the sole of each foot, in the palm of each hand and in different spots throughout our body, these powerful energy centers are where energy flows. When one center is blocked, it is hard for the other energy centers to release tension from the body. Thus, when we behave in a chaotic way, we threaten our bodies. We must realize that each of us was given a gift of choice from the Universal Source of Intelligence. This gift of choice must be utilized to decide which way to direct our energies. It can be solely for the purpose of harmonizing our life form or be at odds within the existence of our being. The easiest way to control our charkas is by using our energy wisely.

Each Chakra has two qualities: one is positive and the other negative, or one is light and the other is dark. However, the two qualities are for you to unfold and become skilled at balancing. The root or base chakra is located in the spine, and its color is red. The functions of the root chakra are to give vitality to the physical body, survival and preservation instinct. If one is positive, the organs flow with liveliness. If one is overly negative, the bodily organs such as the adrenal glands, kidneys and spinal column can be affected negatively. The positive matters relating to the material world include success, uniqueness, stability, security, stillness, health, courage and patience. The negative qualities are anger, greed, violence, insecurity and excessive concern with one's physical survival. What force you pull toward you every second of every minute clearly determines what qualities are pulled out. To keep the forces of nature balanced, you have to work from the inside out. The direction you choose is the energy flow you'll find within yourself, and that determines how you act in any given situation.

The second chakra is close to the navel and is orange. Positive lessons are controlled emotions, non-attached desires, sexual and caring love, change, movement, integration, health, family, tolerance, surrender and melodious, creative working with new ideas and others. The negative physical qualities are overindulgence in food or sex, sexual difficulties, confusion, worthlessness, jealousy, envy, desire to possess, impotence and urine and bladder problems. The bodily organs are ovaries, testicles, spleen and womb. Procreation is the purpose of this chakra. It can be assimilated positively or negatively, depending on you and how you choose to control the forces.

Right above the navel you have the solar plexus and the third chakra, which is yellow. The positive lessons are self-determination, personal strength, mastery of desires, self-discipline, brightness, warmness, awakening, transformation and laughter. The negative qualities are taking in more than one can absorb and concentrating too much force on power and recognition. Anger, fear, hate and digestive disorders are all a part of a negative nature. The bodily organs are the muscles, nervous system, pancreas, adrenals, stomach, gallbladder and liver. The purpose of the solar plexus is to vitalize and center undue anxiety, which affects the sympathetic nervous system, digestive system and emotions. All you have to do is feed your soul with goodness or block your chakra and allow conflict to control you.

The fourth chakra is the heart. The color is pink with

the purpose of attaching the life force from the higher self and energizing the blood flow. The positive qualities are oneness with the all, divine love, forgiveness, kindness, a whole consciousness, peace, trust and harmony. Negative qualities are lack of balance, suppression of love, emotional unsteadiness, heart problems and cut off flow of energy. These are the bodily organs that are affected when you are negative: the heart, thymus gland, flow system, arms, hands and lungs. Take a closer look in the mirror and find out what is causing you to be out of tune with your true nature.

The fifth chakra is the throat. Its purpose is speech, sound vibration and communication. The color is sky blue, and the positive qualities are the power of the spoken word, true communication expressed in speech, writing, arts, truth, knowledge, wisdom, loyalty and honesty. Negative qualities are communication-speech, unwisely used knowledge, communication problems that create ignorance, lack of discernment, depression and thyroid problems. Bodily organs are the throat, mouth and thyroid. Every part of you is what you make it to be. Open your mind and free your soul.

The "third eye" is located in the center of your forehead, between the eyebrows. This one is called the sixth chakra, and the color is indigo. It vitalizes the lower brain and central nervous system. When you're balanced, vision is the light it carries. The positive qualities are intuition, clear insight, positive imagination, clairvoyance, focus and concentration, peace of mind and keen perception. Negative qualities are lack of concentration, fear, tension, headaches, pessimism and extreme disconnection from the world. The organs are the eyes, nose, ears and pituitary gland. Once your third eye is opened, your power is beyond your two eyes. With keen perception, you can look and see through any-thing.

The seventh chakra is the "crown seat." Its color is violet, which is my favorite color. The diadem is located on top of the head. This chakra is the higher self, linked with thought and will. Positive qualities are oneness with the boundless cosmos, unity with the higher self, spiritual strength of will, awareness beyond space and time, realism, service to humanity and love. Negative qualities are lack of inspiration, confusion, depression, alienation, hesitation to serve humanity and senility. The bodily organs are the cerebrum, pineal gland, central nervous system, head and eyes. Oneness with the creator is deep-rooted. We have to keep our crown seat open and let this powerful energy flow and vitalize our existence.

The eighth and ninth energy chakras are not seen with the naked eye. They are the active, higher-level density of who we are, if we can raise our darkness and balance our light. The purpose of these chakras is to fulfill our mission with the universal source and build in ourselves the wholeness of who we really are. Even the vibration and power of sound can lift our spirit to balance out our chakras. Meditation, visualization, affirmation and prayer are vital in balancing our being. This is one of the oldest known ways to strengthen our spirit and connect within. If you like, you can always use candles, incense and flowers to enhance the feeling of calmness.

If you want to be alive in all areas of your life, center and clear your charkas; then, all things will come into place. A crystal-clear mirror of better thoughts will begin to form; a better glow of your soul will begin to immerse with total love, and a better connection with those around you is possible. All you truly need to remember is to store goodness in your soul and enjoy your life's journey.

Maintain your force of wholeness

Now that you know a little about balancing your energies, you must make an effort to remain balanced and sustain your chakras, keep yourself in tune with the spiritual side of you and create a self-disciplined nature to create any reality you choose. If you wish to be successful, you can, as long as you don't scatter your energies in too many directions. If you want to spread joy, express yourself through your abilities and keep an optimistic attitude. Once you have achieved a force of wholeness gained through balancing the forces of nature, which are you, you will live a life in alignment with sincerity, truth and trust. You will be able to express your creativity with total love of others, forgiveness, compassion, peace and harmony.

Here are some of the ways that I maintain wholeness within my being. I make sure that I get an adequate amount of sleep for my well being. I eat fresh fruits, legumes and vegetables. I drink plenty of water to flush impurities out of my temple. I focus on my breathing so I can properly align my soul, spirit, body and mind. I exercise as much as possible. I restore my body through self-healing. I develop my artistic talents daily so that I can share with others and bring an end to situations that no longer serve a useful purpose in my evolutionary process of life.

There are many ways to activate and balance your soul, spirit, mind and body, if you're open to being balanced. When I observe the animal kingdom, the four seasons and the elements of the earth, I find all of these moving forces are aligned with nature. When I observe humans, I find that many of us are out of tune with nature, and other folks don't even care to tune in to their higher vibrations.

As I said before, you are the mirror, and the only way to clean up your double reflection is by connecting with the inner parts of your being and finding more than one way to maintain wholeness. Your mirror can reflect harmonious conditions or distasteful circumstances. Only you can pass the test to shift to the next level that's waiting for you and have the ability to bring about positive energy and vitality. I know that sometimes it's hard to accept the positive and negative to withstand both. However, as long as you have a mind, your greatest weapon to unlock the doors for progress, you must use your positive energy each day to maintain a balance in every area of your life. When you're balanced, you'll know when to hold them and when to fold them. You'll know what is right for you at any given time. You'll know there is a divine force guiding you and directing your path. Let go of all fears; rise above doubts and receive a fresh lifestyle of new ideas and energizing conditions. Draw joyous experiences into your life; create the reality of a balanced and harmonious life, and remember that you are who you create yourself to be.

Once you shift the development of your inner world, the outer world will learn to connect with you through your heart of love, peace, trust and harmony. Naturally the forces of nature, which are you, will become balanced in perfect order. The only thing you must remember is that the forces of nature are the decisions you make.

CHAPTER 9

A CONSTANT FLOW OF CHANGE IN ALL THAT EXISTS THROUGH LOVE, PEACE, TRUST AND HARMONY

Though no one can flow against change, anyone who has a life can change for the better.

Imagine yourself standing in front of the mirror and exploring the beauty of your soul, including anything that appeals to you. What thoughts and images would you choose? Would you choose metaphors that are uplifting or diminishing? Would you choose negative thoughts rather than positive ones? If you are as I am, you probably would choose constructive thoughts. Since you know by now that life is only what you make of it through your pure and unselfish thoughts, there is nothing more elegant than mirroring a life of better thoughts through a constant flow of change through love, peace, trust and harmony.

As beings of great power, we must really begin to recognize that our thoughts are the circumstances of our lives. Before we can flow with life, we must change our unproductive mind-set and align ourselves with all that exists through love. Right now there is a great mental vibration going on in our era that could bring us an enormous amount of love, but only if we are ready to use our minds carefully for constructive purposes. Whether you come to a decision to uplift your thoughts or not is totally up to you. However, anyone who is unable to transform his or her thoughts to a more powerful, beautiful and natural image flows against a life of harmony.

Pull your mind together and stay on the optimistic side of life
Although I've talked about how important it is to change your negative thoughts to positive thinking, we as humans must know that there is always a fine line between positive thoughts and negative ones. I have discovered that when we block out negative thoughts or try to get rid of them, we don't actually eliminate unconstructive thinking. Instead, we get caught up in them even more. The way to pull your mind together and stay on the optimistic side of life is by accepting, acknowledging and healing what is true for you at that time. Let's say you make a negative comment about a person you know. You believe that person has a problem, but you don't. You believe the negative comment you made about that person was justified, true and constructive.

Let's pause for a moment. One of the biggest problems many of us have is we feed into our own negative thoughts without realizing what we are doing. We assume and believe that expressing our feeling about someone else in a negative way is fulfilling, but to put it rather bluntly, what we are doing is not accepting our own ills, deficiencies and negative attitudes. Instead, we regard another with lack and limitations. We believe if we put someone else down, the truth of who we are will not show. We are quick to tell ourselves how inadequate someone else is, instead of acknowledging our own internal issues that need healing. But we must look into our mirror of repressed, deeply embedded hurt and pain and know that our mirror is the negative thoughts and feelings that must be changed.

So often we use words to tear each other and ourselves down without ever realizing what we are doing. I've heard some folks say, "There is no liberty, no fairness or no way out in this world, so why continue to exist?" I've heard others say, "If it weren't for so and so, my life would be a whole lot better." I have realized statements like that pull us away from doing something better with our minds. The world isn't the problem; it is our thinking that causes problems. Instead of holding others responsible for our mental troubles, let's think about owning up to our negative and unchangeable way. Let's use words to cleanse our negative thoughts and emotions. For instance, here are some affirmation words you can use.

- I now release all tendencies to think in ways that hinder my ability to speak words that are beneficial.
- I now accept to think only good and constructive thoughts.
- I always see the loving essence in others.
- I am of health, abundance and harmony.
- I am aware that I can enjoy my life to the fullest.

You can create more affirmations, but remember; you must learn to think constructively and cleanse negative thoughts and emotions when they come to surface.

I know that some people feel comfortable dwelling on negative situations in their lives because they have come accustomed to unsupportive outside influences to shape their world, but when one spends much energy on such reckless thoughts, the individual robs itself of pure energy. If you are a person who cannot connect with the potential of positive thinking through determination, concentration, persistence, enthusiasm, patience and inner peace, your words and thoughts have lost power. Your union with having a clear mind has come against a constant flow of love, peace, trust and harmony because you refuse to pull your life together and build up your mind through every beneficial word you speak.

Our ancestors, the gurus and monks, did not have time to focus on anything negative even though I'm sure that bad things actually happened. However, I know that they had the highest principles to do everything to perfect themselves. I don't think nowadays people put forth enough effort to improve their negative side although life was made for a constant change of achievements and production in one's nature. On the other hand, most people feel uncomfortable conquering their weak spots.

Our thoughts are just as important as every single day of our lives, as well as every single fiber of all that exists. Each person who has ever been a slave to his or her thoughts has power to prevail and pull himself or herself out of wretchedness. If our ancestors have found a way to rope their lives together, then the idea of being pulled by negative thoughts is futile. Personally, I would rather break down the barriers of psychological damages and change my life on a constant basis of expressing the divine flow of love. I do know this frame of mind has helped my life. I am in a positive state of mind living more abundantly and doing the things I enjoy.

If you are open to positive experiences and not afraid to be creative with life, your ultimate goal should be to elevate your thoughts, your vision and ideals. Once you learn to look deep in your heart to draw out the best in you, you'll know how to correct your weaknesses, you'll deal with problems rationally, and you'll understand the positives and negatives of others. The only thoughtful characteristic you need to tug is your strength to enjoy life.

You're one of a kind, so what are you waiting for? Go out and enjoy life

If you want to change your life, then all you need to do is change your mind. I used to feel that some people's lives were so much better than mine and wondered why they seemed to have such a joy for life. To my surprise, I found out after so much pain in my life that they were taking responsibility for their thoughts, setting goals, dreaming big, becoming aware of their feelings and flowing with change by having a positive attitude.

Quite often we humans forget that our destiny is in our own hands. When we lose track of this great force, we cover our mirror with dust, and anyone who knows about dust knows that it sticks around on everything that doesn't get clean. As soon as we take complete control over our minds, then and only then will we be able to wipe the old dust off and enjoy life. I'm certain that you're one of a kind, and it won't take you long to prevail over your thoughts because the wisdom you have acquired symbolizes that you cherish a constant flow of change in all that exists through love, peace, trust and harmony. All you have to do is design the mirror you want and realize that the potent strength of your mind is a well-built force liberated to do whatever you aspire to.

A positive direction will always produce a renewed mind

As long as we can move in a direction of new purposes and plans, the benefits will come into view. Before writing this book, I was in a state of confusion. I felt overwhelmed with moods of worry. It was a difficult struggle to take advantage of my enthusiasm to live life to the fullest until I arrived at a clear decision to change my thoughts and connect to my higher purpose. Time after time, experience has proved to me that as soon as I decide to eliminate turmoil and concentrate on a positive path, I immediately change my mental attitude by getting an enjoyment out of life through a new burst of energy. If I hadn't done that, I might have wallowed in worry, which is a maddening circle of lack of enthusiasm.

Before you start out on your new mental journey of positive direction, I would like to develop a daily program for you that will raise your soul. It is titled "I will live through this day with love."

1. I will live through this day with love because I will keep up with my emotions and actions.

2. I will live through this day with love because I am determined to live in peace.

3. I will live through this day with love so I can concentrate on my aspirations.

4. I will live through this day with love now that I know I can be persistent in fulfilling my dreams.

5. I will live through this day with love because my ability to trust life is through my own thoughts.

6. I will live through this day with love to prepare for good days.

7. I will live through this day with love to work miracles and radiate an inner-warmth and friendliness to everyone I meet.

If you want to write your very own words of inspiration, you can. This is just one of my steps toward more psychological peace. When you think in a positive direction, you will produce a renewed mind. Every part of you will become free and everlasting no matter how depressed, despondent or desperate you are. Trust me; you can change your life through renewing your thoughts and strength every day.

There are benefits to be found in almost anything that happens to you

Sometimes benefits are difficult to see right away, but when you trust the process of a constant flow of change in all that exists through love, peace, trust and harmony, you flow with life. And, since you've come this far despite your past problems or experiences, I'm definite that you've learned something about yourself. If you don't know what that is, I'll tell you. You have learned that change is constant, and within change, you can make choices.

I wanted to end this book without telling another story, but

I have to let you know what just happened. A close friend of mind just called to tell me he had a car accident. He said he was driving forty-five miles per hour in the rain. Suddenly, the car in front of him stopped quickly to make a right turn. Before he could stop, he rear-ended the car. My friend began to shed tears, telling me that he felt sad and confused and that the situation didn't feel real. I asked him if he was okay and if anyone was hurt; he said no. I told him to think about this: he wasn't hurt; no one else was hurt, and the only loss was his car, so he didn't need to sweat the small stuff. He said his car was dented badly, and he was unable to move it. I told him he was where he was supposed to be or he wouldn't have been there. Why worry about spilled milk when you can wipe it up? He replied, "You're right. Let me call the tow truck." As I said before, when something happens to you that is bumpy, change what you can, detach from what you can't and move on to what you can create better for yourself through love, peace, trust and harmony.

I told him to learn from the situation and accept that change is forever constant within you and all around you. Instead of looking at your transformation as being negative, see it like a movie and move away from it. Focus on the positive and form a better plan to release the negative block. Life is an experience of choices. You can choose to overcome obstacles or do nothing. You can recover your attitude or allow attitudes to have power over you. Whatever you decide, you can benefit from almost anything. We only come here to know who and what we are. Have fun with life; don't allow negative situations to take over your being. When you begin to see the bigger picture of who you truly are, you will see that life here on earth is only a school teaching what you need to learn to pass the test of you. I am satisfied to know there is no other way to avoid change when it's ever-present. Just look in the mirror and notice a constant change of you rising, shifting and forming into a better person, but remember first to let loose and hear the atmosphere of greater benefits that start with love. When you reach the pinnacle of love, love is what overpowers conditions and circumstances. Love is what kills hate. Love is what heals wounds and sets you free if you allow it to. I am glad you took time out to read this book. This is my gift to you. Never forget.

Recommended Readings

Maya Angelou, *I Know Why the Caged Bird Sings*

Julia A. Boyd, *Embracing the Fire* and *In the Company of My Sisters*

Les Brown, *It's Not Over Until You Win!*

Deepak Chopra, *Seven Spiritual Laws*

Dawn Marie Daniels and Candace Sandy, *Souls of My Sisters*

Betty J. Eadie, *Embraced by the Light*

Shakti Gawain, *Creative Visualization*

Kahlil Gibran, *The Prophet*

Derrick Hayes, *Derricknyms from A to Z*

Louise Hay, *You Can Heal Your Life, The Power Is Within You*

Shirley MacLaine, *Going Within*

Peter McWilliams, *You Can't Afford the Luxuries of a Negative Thought*

Dr. Judith Orloff, *Guide to Intuitive Healing: Five Steps to Physical, Emotional, and sexual Wellness*

M. Scott Peck, M.D., *The Road Less Traveled*

James Redfield, *The Celestine Prophecy*

Sanaya Roman and Duane Packer, *Opening to Channel*

Denese Shervington and Billie Jean Pace, *Soul Quest*

Pete A. Sanders, Jr., *You Are Psychic!*

Albert Taylor, *Soul Traveler*

Susan Taylor, *In the Spirit*

Iyanla Vanzant, *Acts Of Faith, Yesterday, I Cried* and *In the Meantime*

Elsie Washington, *Uncivil War: The Struggle Between Black Men and Women*

Paramahansa Yogananda, *Scientific Healing Affirmations*

Gary Zukav, *Seat of the Soul* and *Soul Stories*

RESOURCES

More information on how to find help for life's problems.

Professional organizations' web sites
American Academy of Child and Adolescent Psychology:
http://www.aacap.org (1800) 333-7636 Ext. 124

American Psychiatric Association:
http://www.psych.org (202) 682-6000

American Psychological Association:
http://www.helping.apa.org (1800) 964-2000

Anxiety Disorders Association of America:
http://www.adaa.org (301) 231-9350

Co-Dependents Anonymous (CODA):
http://www.codependents.org

National Foundation for Depression Illness, Inc:
http://www.depression.org

Depression-screening:
http://www.depression-screening.org

Freedom From Fear:
http://www.freedomfromfear.com (718) 351-1717

Global Alliance of Mental Illness Advocacy Networks:
http://www.gamian.org (718) 351-1717

Screening for Mental Health, Inc.:
http://www.mentalhealthscreening.org

National Alliance for the Mentally Ill:
http://www.nami.org (1800) 950-6264

National Association of Social Workers:
http://www.naswdc.org (1800) 638-8799

National Depressive and Manic-Depressive Association:
http://www.ndmda.org (1800) 826-3632

National Institute of Mental Health:
http://www.nimh.nih.gov/anxiety

National Mental Health Association:
http://www.nmha.org (1800) 969-6642

Obsessive-Compulsive Foundation:
http://www.ocfoundation.org (203) 878-5669

Each web site provides free information on depression, mood disorders, anxiety, fear and other mental illnesses.

<u>Additional informative self-help web sites with supportive articles and reports</u>
Abundance Institute:
http://www.abundantworld.com

A Free Daily Positive Thought Service:
http://www.free-positive-thought.com

Create Change: http://www.createchange.net

Center for Change: http://www.centerforchange.com

Empowerment Resources:
http://empowermentresources.com

Mind Productions: http://www.mindpro.com

Objective Happiness: http://www.objectivehappiness.com

Powerfully Recovered:
http://www.powerfullyrecovered.com

Self Esteem Advisory Service:
http://www.selfesteemadvisoryservice.com

Self-Growth: http://www.selfgrowth.com

Self-Help Website Database: http://www.iqtest.com/se/

Spirit Site: http://www.spiritsite.com

Spiritual Light Journeys:
http://www.spirituallightjourneys.com

<u>Spiritual Institutions</u>
Inner Visions Worldwide Network:
http://www.innervisionsworldwide.com

Omega Institute for Holistic Studies: http://www.eomega.org

Earth Healing: http://www.earthhealing.com

Order additional copies

To order additional copies of *The Mirror is You*,
please fill out the form below and mail with your payment to
Vibexpress Publishing, LLC, P.O. Box 83083, Conyers, GA 30013

Orders may also be placed online at www.siddiyaswift.com

Please make checks payable to Vibexpress Publishing, LLC

Qty. _____   X $11.95 USA/$16.95 CAN = **$** _____

Ground shipping $4.50

Total $_____

If paying by credit card, please complete the following section.

☐ Mastercard ☐ Visa
Name as it appears on card _____
Card number _____ exp. _____

Name _____

Organization _____

Address _____

Phone _____ Fax _____

email_____

We hope you enjoyed this Vibexpress publication.
If you would like to receive monthly newsletters featuring additional
Vibexpress products and services, please contact
Vibexpress Publishing, LLC
P.O. Box 83083
Conyers, GA 30013
Phone: 770-388-0769 Fax: 770-388-0253
email: publishing@siddiyaswift.com

Please visit the Vibexpress Publishing website at
www.siddiyaswift.com